DOLPHINS INTO THE FUTURE

JOAN OCEAN

A Dolphin Connection Book
Hawaii
1997

DOLPHINS INTO THE FUTURE

A Dolphin Connection Book

First Printing, 1997

Copyright © 1997 by Joan Ocean

Cover Art: Jean-Luc Bozzoli ©
Layout, Editing, and Design: Suchi Psarakos
Imaging: Kym L. Miller, Scott Matsushiga, Alex Unabia, Belknap Imaging, Hawaii
Printing: Thomson-Shore Inc., Dexter, Michigan

Library of Congress Catalog Card Number: 97-76735

ISBN: 0-9625058-8-9

Published in the United States by
Dolphin Connection
P.O. Box 275
Kailua, Hawaii, USA 96734

DEDICATION

I dedicate this book with deep Love and Gratitude
to the friendly Hawaiian Spinner dolphins of Pods A, B and C:

Exx, Two Wave, Dimple, Line, Stitches, Crater I (male), Parallel, Crater II (female), Fancy, Three Spot, Tippy, Wrinkley, Tattered Fin, Bumps, Cookie, Comb, Swirl, Zac, Wave, Bentley, Notches, Ragged Fin, Blunted Fluke, No Mark, Dragonfly, Ramrod, Two I.V. (inverted waves), Diamond, Old Scar, Paint, Crochet, Double You, Nickers, Pacmom and baby, Blip, Finger, Beauty Mark, Three I.V., Whitey, Feather, Ivy, Two Nicks, Mesa, Pyramid, Singer, Friendly, Remora Kid, Exclamation, Hi Brow, Sunburst, Black Scratches, Blemy, Peter, Patches, Baby Arrow, "M", Army Sergeant, Triangle Eye, White Mark, Snubnose, Pseudo-Zac, January, Two Bites, Crooked Fin, Wishbone, Book Ends (2), Curly and Curly Q, Unicorn, Lumpy, Lace, Two Notch, The Twins, Button, Seaweed Mouth, RCA, Remora Port, Can Opener, Corky, Moonsmile, Scalloped Dorsal, Little Bit, Flat Dimple, Slice, Chevron, Propeller Gash, Tatoo, Puck, Baby White Stripes, S.A. (South America), Baby James, White Stripe, Fangs, Scooter, Scissors, P.S. (Peace Sign), Yarn, Sirius, Candle, Echo, UFO, Feisty, Holey, Spot, Varicose Kid, Snippet, Bubbles, Queen, Speedy, Motley, Kaikea, Peduncle Dash, Fantail, "H", Watermark, Radio, Popcorn, Jumping Baby, Twister, Patch Eye, Staple, Flower, Dottie, Na Pali, Dancer, Cameo, Cave, Parentheses, Horseshoe, Sliver, Singalong, Shape Shifter,
And all the rest...

IN GRATITUDE

I am grateful to the following people
who have been my source of love, inspiration and joy:

Agnes and Cyril Phillips, my parents; Lisa Joan Garrison, Laura Carole and Frank Joseph Garofalow, my children; Tom Garrison, Elvira Garofalow, Miranda Grace, Nathaniel Thomas, Lindsay Gabrielle and all my grandchildren.

Suchi Psarakos, dolphin researcher, who edited this book with gentle sensitivity, exceptional awareness and endless humor. She knows the Spinners as well as I do.

My friends and pod ners: John W. Float, John C. Lilly, Jean-Luc Bozzoli, Ken Kimura, Virginia Coyle, Jim and Katy Nollman, Evelyn Phillips Thompson, Lorraine Phillips O'Grady, Tim O'Grady, Charles and Dawn Phillips, Gowri Motha, Scott and Johnnie Jones, Seyril Schochen, Lanakila Brandt, Miriam F. Baker, Bonnie Vrooman, Trish and Wally Franklin, Kamala Hope-Campbell, Claire Leimbach, Irene van Lippe-Biesterfeld, Elizabeth Eason, Yurika Nozaki, Chris Reid, Inta Rudajs, Trish Regan, Doug Hackett, Patricia Hooper, Elaine Thompson, Jack Davis, Rebecca Fitzgerald, Peter Insalaco, Claudia and Kevin Merrill, Jeff and Terry Leicher, Horace Dobbs, Denise Herzing, Dorothy Spero, Robbins Barstow, Bill Rossiter, Kinsley Jarrett, John and Janette, JoAnn, Kitty, Krista, Saskia, Dawn, Cindy, Chuck, James, Tina, Mark, Lara, Val, Micky, Linda, Rashani, Bob, Debbie, Pomaikai, Lorn, Cam, Nancy, Angela, Chelsea and all the many wonderful helpers, pod-leaders and participants of the Hawaiian dolphin-ocean swims.

I also acknowledge the love and guidance of my friends from other planets and other dimensions. We are united in a love for humanity and all the Beings created in God's image.

Also by Joan Ocean:

Dolphin Connection: Interdimensional Ways of Living
Open to the Sea (video)

The photographs in this book were taken by:

Jean-Luc Bozzoli
Joan Ocean
Shuhei Okada
Suchi Psarakos
Lorn Douglas
Jaynellen Kovacevich
Victoria Cotton and Kim Kindersley, still from *The Dolphin's Gift*,
    Zari Productions ©

TABLE OF CONTENTS

INTRODUCTION

April 17, 1990

Swimming in the bay, I see five streamlined dolphins, appearing like silver cylinders in the depths below. As they slowly move ahead, another group of six dolphins fluke gently into their place directly beneath me while I float on the surface. The five dolphins ahead are slowly rising upward. The six below pivot up toward me, three of them looking at me now, their beaks pointing directly at me, their eyes visible on the sides of their heads. They see me and they sonar me...high-pitched steady clicking that resonates throughout my body. Are they telling me they are coming up? Are they checking to see if I am a friend or foe? Are they asking why I don't come down and join them?

Never wanting to interfere, I sense their direction of movement and slowly roll to one side, clearing a space above them as they gently rise. They appear unconcerned by my presence. A mere flick of their tails and they could swim away. Together they slowly float upward next to me and we spout in unison. We swim and breathe together. I am one of them, a member of the pod. Deep Love, deep blue. Breathe, fluke, fluke...breathe, fluke, fluke... breathe, fluke, fluke, fluke. Now diving together, they go deeper than I, but as one group still, they swim along the bottom while I swim above. What is their message? *"Enjoy yourself my friend. We know you well."*

The dolphins are calling us into the ocean. They want to meet us, to introduce us to their world and to swim with us into the unknown. They are intelligent friends who exemplify qualities we value — cooperation, harmony, peace, joyfulness, good health, beauty, wisdom, supple movement, grace and unconditional love. The dolphins and whales are approaching us around the globe, filling our minds with visions of freedom, and interacting with us to encourage us to attain many life-enhancing qualities.

I am a counseling psychologist by training and I have understood from the beginning of my human/dolphin connection that experiences with the dolphins and whales are teachings about human potentials and spiritual unfoldment. The calling that I have received from the cetaceans is a call to people about our unlimited essence and our capacity to experience love more fully.

This is what the dolphins have been showing me by their example as I swim with them almost every day. It has changed my life and it has affected the community of friends who live in my neighborhood and swim with me. In this book I will share with you the teachings of the dolphins and whales.

I have traveled to numerous locations to meet them — joining them in the Bay of Bengal in India, Sea of Java in Bali, Sea of China, Sea of Cortez, the Bahamas, Monkey Mia and Hervey Bay, Australia, the Canary Islands, the Hawaiian Islands, the Indian Ocean, the Red Sea, Israel, Egypt, Canada and the Amazon River.

Ironically, one of my greatest assets as I began this work was being a novice in the water. In 1984 when I first timidly entered the ocean to see some bottlenose dolphins, I didn't know how to swim. In fact, as I wrote in my first book, *Dolphin Connection: Interdimensional Ways of Living*, I had a deeply ingrained fear of the ocean. However, because I was a newcomer to the ocean, it was easy for me to enter the water as a "student" of the dolphins and be open to experiencing their knowledge.

Since 1989 I have lived with three pods, or families, of more than two hundred wild Hawaiian Spinner dolphins, *Stenella longirostris*. I have logged over six thousand hours in the water — listening to the dolphins, watching them, mimicking them, filming, recording, documenting them and enriching my own life because of them. I have learned that cetaceans communicate in a way that requires an entirely different mind set than the human cognitive-thinking model. Rather than in words and sentences, dolphins communicate through vibrations, through sonar and synchronized movement, through acoustic images, feelings, sounds, and group-energy fields. They work with the electromagnetic grids of the planet, using these underwater pathways to send messages for miles beneath the sea.

They know how to access multiple dimensions. This means they are simultaneously experiencing life in the ocean and life in an ontological world of multi-level subtle realities. As they swim with me, I am often fascinated by their ability to be wonderful three-dimensional, physical friends, while they also interact with vibrational holograms that take them to fourth and fifth-dimensional worlds. They serve as inspirational examples to us of the possibilities existing beyond our present belief systems.

What they are doing, and what they are teaching us, is *exactly* what we humans will be doing in the twenty-first century. This is why there is such a yearning in people to be with dolphins and to learn from them — we sense the importance and the timeliness of their wisdom.

In 1988 I was guided to move to Hawaii where I was told I would make physical, real-life contact with extraterrestrials (ETs). Of course I thought the message meant I would meet with human entities from other planets. Although that eventually happened too, now I understand that the original channeling referred to the dolphins and whales and counted on my interest in ETs to motivate me to relocate to Hawaii, where my vibrational communication work was to begin.

The dolphins and whales are "extraterrestrials." They do not live on land, on terra firma, they live in the ocean...so they are "extra" terrestrials. Theirs is a different environment from our own. When we immerse ourselves in the ocean for hours, we are transported into another dimensional world. Everything we see and feel is new and unknown, relative to our earthbound lives. As we swim along we see the blueness ahead of us. We see shapes and forms moving in the current before us. We look ahead and we cannot see our own bodies. It feels like free-floating in outer space!

In addition to living in another world, the Hawaiian Spinner dolphins are at One with nature. They live in a state of Love that suspends judgment, anger and retaliation, and their abilities to use more of their physical, sensory, and intelligence potentials reminds us that we can do that too. The dolphins operate out of a different paradigm than the human race. They have not been raised in a culture that requires primarily rational thinking. They know there is much more than that. We can learn their ways and enrich ourselves. As we broaden our attitudes, the physiology of our bodies will change also. There are many wonderful adventures awaiting our entrance into the dolphin world.

As humans we want happiness — the dolphins have found this. We want peace of mind — when you swim with wild dolphins, you find it with them. We want beauty and love — the dolphins create them vibrationally, shaping their own habitats. They feel vibrations, create holographic works of art all around themselves and then play among them.

These are the experiences I will share with you in this book, in the hope that some of the ideas and skills of the dolphins will inspire you to take these studies further and develop them into healing modalities for people and our planet. The dolphins have taken me through a very precise and methodical "course of study," compelling me to open to their wisdom and set aside my old limiting beliefs about who I am as a human being on Earth at this time in the history of the Universe. They have helped me expand into near and distant worlds.

In writing this book, I am creating a multi-informational experience for the reader. Some of the stories taken directly from my daily journals from 1989 to 1997 are not presented chronologically, rather they are shared where appropriate to further explain a concept about the dolphins' teachings. Some are about the dolphins being the physical, three-dimensional ocean mammals we see and believe in. Other stories reveal the dolphins' advanced propensities to expand their minds and convert matter into refined fields of energy beyond the five senses presently familiar to people. These stories are intermingled, reproducing the "dolphin experience" of an expansive holographic communication that takes us into whole-brain living. In reading this book you can bridge multiple realities and awaken unexplored levels of your mind.

I look forward to swimming with you in these joyful Realms of Light.

Joan Ocean
Hawaii, 1997

HAWAIIAN SPINNER DOLPHINS

A s a spiritual and caring person, I sensed that I was incarnated on Earth for a reason, but that reason seemed to elude me. In 1989 I realized that I had within me the ability to revise my present reality and use my emotionally charged thoughts, my love and compassion, to create whatever life my mind could comfortably accept as possible for me. BUT — what did I want?

CHOOSING A NEW LIFE

With this in mind, I sat down to write a story to create my new life. In this story, I visualized myself living in a large, comfortable home, surrounded by nature and located on land that changed from green lawns to blue ocean. From my backyard, I could enter the water and easily live among the sea creatures. I visualized dolphins there.

Within two weeks of writing that vision, my friend and world-renowned environmentalist, Dexter Cate, called me, suggesting I visit the Big Island of Hawaii, where he had swum among the local, Hawaiian Spinner dolphins.

I flew from Oahu to the Big Island, and there I saw dozens of dolphins swimming close to shore. I was a novice swimmer and normally did not stay in the water very long, but as the pod swam towards me, I quietly treaded water and watched them pass. It was wonderful to see so many beautiful, graceful dolphins with their attractive charcoal gray and white coloring, effortlessly gliding by with hardly a glance. I was happy to be in their presence.

After many hours passed, I felt chilled and thirsty so I swam to shore and walked the quiet, narrow beach road to my parked car. En route I passed a house with green hedges and purple flowers and a "For Rent" sign. Forgetting my fatigue, I inquired within, entering the house that has now become my home and center for communication research with dolphins. Eventually I learned that this same house had been occupied by cetacean biologist Dr. Ken Norris and other dolphin researchers during their interesting and preliminary studies of wild dolphins in this location. Initially I rented the home for a week, and then another week, and then a month, until I finally moved here permanently. Interestingly, even before I moved here it was called "Dolphin House." It matched exactly the house I had visualized. The next phase of my spiritual work was about to begin.

Beginning my new life in this home, I was happy to be with the fish, the birds and the eels. The dolphins did not visit every day, but I was learning how to swim in the ocean, strengthening my arms and legs and enjoying the soft salty water that allowed me to float and dream for hours. I was financially supported by friends who rented rooms in the house and the sales of my first book and the Dolphin Connection visionary notecards that had provided an income for my partner, Jean-Luc Bozzoli, and me for our years of traveling to many countries sharing our dolphin experiences and visionary art. Now we swam together every day and watched to see what the dolphins would do.

DOLPHIN TEACHERS

The first time I saw a pod of thirty-five wild dolphins swimming in the water near my new home, I was overjoyed. I couldn't believe my good luck and my heart filled with gratitude for the fulfillment of my longtime dream. They swam fast, focussed on each other, with very little interest in me. I didn't care. I was happy to be in the same water with them. I felt honored by their presence and inspired by the sight of their sleek, graceful bodies moving in synchronicity through the warm autumn waters. As they surfaced, the sun glittered on their fins and I heard the multiple spouting sounds of their breathing before they dove below again.

I had been raised on the east coast in the United States and had never considered swimming in the Atlantic Ocean (although I understand some people do it!) The water there seemed cold and turbulent. I had been content to sit on the beach and enjoy its rhythms and beauty from a distance.

Now the appeal of the dolphins and the friendliness of this gentle, Hawaiian bay persuaded me to learn to swim and to strengthen my swim strokes every day. My friend Elizabeth relocated from Oahu near me. As I watched Elizabeth swim so naturally and gracefully, she gave me confidence. I began to appreciate the ocean for the first time in my life.

Each day I swam a little farther and my aquatic self-confidence grew. I became more comfortable with the water and the mask and snorkel. I felt ready for the dolphins to teach me more. They swam closer, eying me inquisitively, the occasional juvenile darting over to swim next to me before rejoining the pod. There were approximately thirty-five dolphins in this pod in December, 1989. They escorted me at a distance of twenty feet, maintaining the same direction and tempo as I was. I was aware of them, but if I tried to swim directly toward them, they swam away. With a flick of their tails, they could easily be gone! I had read in Hawaiian literature about Spinner dolphins.

They were known to be extremely shy of divers and seldom allowed themselves to be photographed underwater. This seemed true.

As they swam by I made note of their markings, and when I returned to shore I drew their pictures carefully in a log book. I soon recognized the same dolphins were returning to swim in the bay. Their presence made me feel safe, and consequently I swam farther and farther from shore when they were there. It was like a meditation. In the early morning hours when the bay was empty of boats and swimmers, I could dream and be silent to my heart's content. I was able to clear my mind of all concerns.

GETTING TO KNOW YOU

Within two months I felt that the dolphins had come to know and trust me. I noticed that there were different groups of dolphins frequenting the bay. Eventually I learned that there were at least three distinct pods, usually comprised of thirty-five to forty-seven dolphins each. I named these dolphin groups Pod A, Pod B and Pod C. Most of the dolphins had marks on their bodies that were recognizable when they swam nearby. Based on these birthmarks and healed wounds, I started naming the dolphins: Tattered Fin, Exx, Blunted Fluke, Ragged Fin, Whitey, Crater, Wave, Two Wave, Notches, Scar, Paint, Tippy, Three Spot, Bentley, Baby Bumps, Dimple, Wrinkley, Zac, Comb, Arrow, Thimble (or Finger), Singer, Lace, Button, Pacmom, Beauty Mark, Curly, Blip and Crochet. Some were more interested in me than others; Pod A showed the most interest.

Through the years, I have identified and named over two hundred dolphins traveling in four different pods. Within these pods there are certain dolphins who are "human/dolphin ambassadors." They are the group in each pod who repeatedly make contact with swimmers. There does not seem to be any dolphin pod leader. Often a group of five, six or seven males arrives first and spends hours swimming with us, but that does not stop the other pod members from joining in. I always have the choice to swim with whichever dolphin group I prefer. Sometimes in the interest of befriending some of the newcomers, I choose to observe the more quiet, reserved members of the pod and leave the playful dolphins for the other swimmers to enjoy. There is so much to see and experience each day with the dolphins.

November 27, 1993

This morning as I look into the by, I see many dolphins playing on the surface near the shore. I hurry into my swimsuit and have a quick cup of tea. I know the dolphins are ready to play and I am filled with anticipation for our wonderful morning. My friend, James, and I swim out at a steady but leisurely pace. I know to conserve my energy for what's to come. The bay is suddenly quiet. I continue to swim to the place in the bay where I regularly meet with the dolphins. They are no longer near the shore and there are no fins in sight. This is so typical. They often seem to completely disappear for five or ten minutes when anyone arrives in the bay. Are they sonaring us and determining whether to join us or not? Then, predictably, they appear out of nowhere beneath us, looking up and rising to the surface to surround us with their love and accept us into their pod.

Now I am totally lost among them. They are above me, beneath me, side by side, in front and behind. I am surrounded and so happy to see my old friends. Wow! There are so many! I see members of Pod A. "Hi, dear friends, so glad to see you again." There is *Fancy* and *Paint* and *Exx* and *Dimple, Line, Stitches, Crater, Bumps, Crochet, Cookie, Comb, Swirl* and *Scratches*. And now I see Pod B is here too. What a great reunion! There's the happy quartet, *Zac, Ragged Fin, Notches* and *No Mark* coming alongside me to say hello. There's *Blunted Fluke* and *Nickers, Bentley, Three I.V., Army Sergeant, Sunburst, Ramrod, Pseudo-Zac* and *Queen. Pyramid* is there and there's a dolphin I see only about four times a year. This dolphin was originally named by Dr. Ken Norris and photographed by his research associates in 1979. When I met the dolphin I named him *Thimble*, but later deferred to Dr. Norris's name of *Finger*. He has most of his dorsal fin missing with only an upright piece about two fingers wide still remaining. He is a large old dolphin who usually swims in the company of other males.

A juvenile is here with a new wound. By the deeply carved cuts on her fluke it looks like a propeller caught her tail briefly. The right end of her fluke is hanging off, still attached by some skin, and as she moves her tail, I see the underside has fresh scars on it. They reflect bright white skin in the blue water, making her easily identifiable from a distance. I name this dolphin *Speedy*, after the speed boat that nicked her. An adult female swims close by her side, allowing *Speedy* to ride in her water flow field and keep her balance.

Now *Three Spot* comes by with *Scooter*, *Wave* and *Scissors*. They invite me to dive with them and we grace-fully jackknife, fluke down, spin underwater and parallel swim together under the surface. On the surface we remain together while we skim the water and breathe in unison, weaving among each other. Sometimes I think I'd like to touch their smooth, muscular skin, but even think-ing the thought creates a slight change in their position, an inch further away. They read my thoughts. The touch-ing only occurs under their discretion, by their choice. They swim against me and touch my arms with their sides.

Everywhere I look, there are dolphins. I am having a wonderful, joyful swim with a group of twenty-five dolphins, my "pod-ners." I wonder where James and the other swimmers are. Later I learn that they are each enjoying themselves with other dolphin groups. There are so many dolphins today. I wonder how many. In my head I am trying to guess numbers based on the dolphins I have seen who I know. The dolphins seem to read my mind. Suddenly all the dolphins are swimming below me in an orderly spread formation. Quickly I count each adult and baby. One hundred fourteen! All of Pod A and Pod B are here, plus some others I don't know.

One dolphin swims over the top of another one and puts her pectoral fins on each side of the second dolphin's head, caressing him repeatedly, as if to give him a head and neck massage! Now ten dolphins are moving as one mass, as close together as they can get. They seem to be trying to become one, tying themselves in a knot. They swim up to James and he is included in the midst of their tight-knit group.

Singer is an active juvenile who loves to swim with people. She makes loud, high-pitched, insistent sounds and a stream of bubbles trails behind her endlessly as she zooms around. She comes over to James and I, darting between us as if to weave the three of us together. Very excited, she travels at high speed from surface to sand, comes up from below as if she will crash into us, then propels herself back and forth on the bottom, releasing an assortment of bubbles, creating a field of bubble "sentences." When we imitate her excited swimming and diving behavior, she responds with great enthusiasm as if we are the most entertaining creatures around.

Other dolphins are making bubbles too. *Fancy* releases two large, fifteen-inch bubbles which glisten in the sun as they rise to the surface. My friend Ken has just arrived. He swims over and hovers above them, letting them break on his solar plexus. *Fancy* dives and releases a barrage of smaller ones. I dive into her stream of bubbles, expel the air in my lungs to imitate her behavior and release a burst of bubbles from my snorkel. Three dolphins turn back and swim over to see what's happening and swim through my bubble wall.

I notice two of this season's babies swimming together. They are diving and surfacing in tandem. So small, so perfect. Wondering who their mother is, I watch them in admiration as they swim next to me. I see one adult female taking care of them. She escorts them wherever they swim, and occasionally nips at their quickly passing flukes. Later in the morning I observe this same trio. The two babies are definitely in the care of one female and she is nursing both of them. I don't think they are twins because I did not see any twins born this year. I wonder where the other adult might be and if this female is a mother or a wet nurse.

There were six dolphins born to Pod B in the Fall of 1993 — two in September, three in October and one in November. I haven't seen Pod A in the bay since September 27th, and they had no new births at that time. Now I see three tiny new babies with the pod, certainly born this month, probably born this week. They are so skinny and only sixteen inches long. They swim very close to their mothers, hardly visible beneath their bellies.

One dolphin has the name *Baby James* because he was born in 1993 on my friend's birthday, June 24. It was not the normal birthing month for this pod and he appeared to be premature. Being born earlier, he is more active than the other babies his age. We all laugh at his antics, very daring for such a tiny fellow. He often propels himself across the bay in a leaping frenzy, on his own and separate from the pod. This morning we watch him make an amazing leap out of the ocean and execute it perfectly. Usually baby dolphins wiggle and squirm as they jump out of the water. They are just learning to control and master their bodies. But *Baby James* thrills us all with his incredible, flying, fifteen-foot leaps into the sky! Later, he treats me to a view of his technique. He swims alongside me, gives me a deep meaningful look, plummets down to the bottom, curves upward before touching the sand, begins strong fluke strokes, and then propels himself straight up, through the water's surface into the air. He flies so high. We are so proud of him. So precocious and clever!

Baby January is here also. She is very happy to swim with people and is easily identified by a small cookie cutter shark bite on her left side. She received this soon after her birth in January, 1993. A remora fish was attached to her for six months but now has left and she seems fine. You can tell that she was raised among human swimmers. She swims so close and is so independent, I'm sure she thinks I'm a dolphin relative!

We dive and circle together, swimming with arms at our sides so as not to startle them. The dolphins respond with great joy to our human attempts to be as graceful and agile as they are.

TWO WAVE

As a beginning swimmer, the dolphins trained me to increase my endurance in the water by including me in lengthy swims. Every day they arrived, I swam among them for two to three hours. I quickly determined which pod had come and what mood they were in. Sometimes the dolphins were quiet and swimming beneath me in a spread formation, other times they were exuberantly playful, jumping and splashing on the surface. These play-days were always the most fun and caused me to expend more energy than I thought I had. And yet somehow I never felt tired, only energized by the interactions.

The dolphins were irresistible. Even now, when I see them leaping out of the water — they are calling me, I must go! I instinctively mimic their behaviors as best I can and this includes deep diving. Having learned to free dive in 1989, it still took great effort on my part to do this. Kicking to get down beneath the surface exhausted me and I immediately had to come back up to gasp for a breath of air. After years of being afraid of sinking and drowning, now I wondered if I'd ever learn to remain underwater!

But the dolphins would have none of that. They assigned me a special dolphin to improve my diving skills. This was *Two Wave*, my beautiful dolphin diving instructor.

Two Wave received her name because of two wavelike markings where the charcoal gray met the light gray shade on her right flank. She was friendly from the first day we met, and had endless patience with all swimmers in her determination to meet everyone beneath the waves. She swam with me for two years, September 10, 1989 to September 10, 1991 and then disappeared! Her work with me was finished. Nevertheless I still look for her, and hope someday I'll see those familiar two wave markings again. Thanks dear friend for all the fun, for your patience and love.

September 3, 1991

At 6:12 a.m. the pod arrives. They wake me from a deep morning sleep by entering my dream state. I become aware of a great excitement inside myself and without looking toward the bay, I know it is my favorite pod, impatiently awaiting my arrival. I'm in the water immediately, and sure enough, there is my sweet friend, *Two Wave*. She swims quickly to me and we begin playing together, swimming in small circles, round and round. Such joy! We are so happy to see each other.

Soon three lovely women visiting from Japan come to join us in the water. Jean-Luc is there and my friend, JoAnn. We swim with Pod A, who treat all the swimmers to the same close encounters. I learned from the beginning that the dolphins respond to most people equally, and it is pointless to become possessive of them. The dolphins are friendly with everyone who approaches them gently. It's an exemplary trait.

The water is wonderfully clear today and the friends from Japan are amazed by how close to us the dolphins swim. I slow down to watch as *Two Wave*, with great patience and perseverance, swims side by side with JoAnn and then Mitsuyo and then Yushi and then Yuriko, staying close, making eye contact and then diving slowly. She dives shallowly alongside them over and over again, obviously inviting them to join her. I watch with surprised amusement as the three Japanese swimmers, who entered the deep water with much apprehension, receive *Two Wave*'s message. They cannot resist her appealing invitation, and they attempt their first dives. I know what *Two Wave* is doing, so I smile and observe the interaction as I swim slowly behind. Mitsuyo splashes and kicks on the surface attempting to follow *Two Wave* under the water.

Two Wave spouts, swims alongside them, and makes another shallow dive, showing them exactly how to do it. The women try again and soon they are elated with the success of their first dives. *Two Wave* seems very pleased as she circles around them. Jean-Luc captures it on film. Then *Two Wave* rejoins me and we are off swimming playfully together, weaving back and forth, diving and spouting as we go.

Now *Two Wave* stays very close and remains on the surface for a long time. Perhaps she is transmitting information to me, because I suddenly understand how I can remain under water longer. I realize that the dolphins surface and breathe often. It is like hyperventilating! It expands the lung capacity. I begin taking many short breaths before diving deep. It works! I can remain underwater with *Two Wave* for a longer time. Now I have a new technique to use and increase my below-surface time. I continue to practice as we swim on and on together. We spend five hours swimming, diving and playing before I return home.

Some of *Two Wave*'s diving lessons with me are captured on the Dolphin Connection video, *Dolphin Connection: Open To The Sea*.

DIVES AND SPINS

Most swimmers who join the dolphins in the bay are sensitive, aware people who respect the lifestyle of the dolphins. They know that the dolphins dive in different ways depending on their mood and activities. It is helpful to observe dolphin behavior and then understand what they are doing, and how to be with them without interrupting their sleep and play.

Sometimes the entire pod of dolphins swims in a spread formation in a quiet and methodical way. They usually breathe and dive together in groups of eight or twelve. In spread formation they inhale and exhale three breaths above water and then make an abrupt dive straight down toward the ocean floor. They are resting. If you want to join them in these regularly timed dives it is good to move silently and gracefully so as not to disturb their pattern. If you continue to swim with them, you will notice the rhythm of their spouts and dives. They will not respond to your overtures to play with them, they are in a quiet, meditative mood. However they seem quite content to have you join them in their meditation. Often when they are quiet like this and they swim up to me, they have their eyes closed. Sometimes our longest and closest swims occur when they escort me for hours in this peaceful, meditative state.

Conversely, when the dolphins want to play, they swim next to you, individually making eye contact, and after a few breaths they slowly make a shallow, spiraling dive. They look at you as they dive, turning their body sideways to watch how you respond. They are inviting you to dive alongside them and they move slowly to accommodate you. As their diver-companion, you are to gracefully jackknife beside them, keeping your arms at your side if possible so as not to startle them or disturb the gentle movement they are initiating. Of course during days of more rambunctious playtime, the dolphins, especially the juveniles, may do successions of quick dives around you, still shallow and spiraling, but also energetic and joyful. These dives bring out a more playful and athletic response in you, where you also attempt multiple quick dives to compliment theirs. Splashing and flying fins are okay! In these situations, anything goes!

When a fast-moving boat or something unexpected enters their path, the dolphins often dive suddenly. You can feel the urgency of these dives. They are no longer focused on your presence, something else has entered their field. At these times I always look up to see what has caused this reaction. It can be as simple as additional swimmers heading their way or a zodiac coming to see them. Often the dolphins prefer to observe changes in their immediate environment from beneath the surface. Repeatedly I have observed dolphins (and whales) dive when boats or people approach them. However it is not necessarily a negative reaction to the boat or people; they prefer to sonar the people and listen to the approaching boat from the depths of the water where they can sense, echolocate and hear better what is happening in the water. As soon as they have determined what is approaching, they return to the surface, and in the case of boats some dolphins in the pod choose to ride the boat's bow wave. Rarely have I seen them intimidated by boats or people after their initial verification.

Spinner dolphins are amazingly acrobatic and adept at aerial spinning. They project themselves out of the water with powerful thrusts of energy that spiral them with dizzying speeds clockwise and counterclockwise, somersaulting and "walking on water" with their flukes. They also leap in the air for joy and certainly for the psychedelic experience of spinning at high speed in midair on clear bright days, watching the world go by. I have also observed adult dolphins demonstrating aerial spins to baby dolphins and encouraging them to mimic these jumps. Baby dolphins often practice their aerial spins when they are merely two hours old.

Sometimes you may see a single dolphin make a fast dive to the bottom. She then turns and propels herself to the surface for an aerial leap out of the water. This is very powerful and impressive to watch from below the surface as well as above. The dolphin moves fast and effortlessly. Deep dives are not essential for all aerial spins since dolphins can also use their flukes and make these leaps from the surface.

REMORAS

I have watched the dolphins spin out of the water in attempts to dislodge remora sucker fish that are attached to their bodies. Remoras eat parasites from the skin of the dolphins and are tolerated initially. However they often remain on a dolphin's body, make it their home, and soon eat away layers of skin, leaving raw, open wounds. Swimming among the dolphins so frequently, I have even had remoras attach themselves to my leg or arm. Treading water or swimming slowly, they are benign; but when I swim fast and dive deeply, they grip tightly to my skin and become quite painful. Fortunately I have hands to remove them. Contrary to what one might think, the dolphins do not remove them from each other. Even when I once tried to help a dolphin, the remora moved so quickly I could not get a grip on it. So sometimes a dolphin will try to dislodge a remora by hurling himself into the air and falling onto the side where it is attached. It occasionally works and the dislocated remora swims freely, looking for another body to latch on to!

I have also seen the dolphins use aerial spins as a signal to the rest of the pod. The particular sound created by the resounding slap of their bodies as they hit the water's surface appears to relay a variety of messages that can be heard over long distances. They can land on their flat flank with a reverberating, high profile wallop, reenter the water head-first making a more subtle splash, or reenter fluke first after somersaulting in midair.

DOLPHIN LIFE

As time passed, I observed the dolphins frequenting the bay by my home an average of twenty days per month, year round. At the end of each day, the pods swim into the deeper waters of the ocean where they spend the night, feeding. While in these deep waters, the dolphins are prey to Cookie Cutter Sharks, small eight to twelve inch fish that move at incredible speeds and take a cookie-shaped hole of flesh out of the dolphin's body. Many dolphins have these wounds and sometimes complications and infections set in which can make the dolphin ill. It is especially upsetting to see a baby dolphin with a cookie cutter bite. The babies are a lighter, white color for the first month and become favorite targets of these small, fast sharks. Here is a picture of Crater with a cookie cutter shark bite on his right flank.

Most of the births occur in the waters close to shore between August and March each year. Usually they are born fluke first, spiraling out of their mothers' wombs. Then they are escorted to the surface for their first breath of air. The babies are interested in people and are very curious. Approximately sixteen to eighteen inches long at birth, they are slender, wrinkled and uncoordinated for the first day. Because of this it is easy to recognize a newborn. They swim against their mother's bellies, almost looking like large remoras attached to the side of the female dolphin. After only a week of nursing they become more rounded and robust. I often observe the babies nursing from more than one female in the pod.

September 19, 1997

Swimming in the bay today I am greeted by a group of nineteen Pod C Spinners. I am overjoyed to see three newborns, one of them with our dolphin friend, *Pacmom*. I beam my love to *Pacmom* and her new baby, feeling like a grandmother! I reflect on the date, realizing it is the beginning of the birthing season, September. These babies are still so tiny and wobbly, barely visible against the sides of their mothers, they must be less than a day old. All of Pod C swims together in a supportive way, allowing space for each little one to surface often for air before quickly wiggling down to mom's side again.

As I swim along, my eye catches a dolphin beneath me jerking in an unusual way. Looking down I am amazed to see a birth in progress! A tiny dolphin is abruptly propelled from the mom's vaginal vent, amid white flecks and liquid foam. Taking only a moment to acclimate himself, the newborn quickly heads for the surface, followed by his mom, who appears a bit concerned that the little one may get away from her. How fast he swims directly to the surface for air, mom following about two feet behind. Taking a breath, his mom moves alongside him. He is safe in her slip stream.

Swimming beside them, admiring the latest member of the pod, I am then astonished to see *Two Nicks* about thirty feet away from me — giving birth! Not as clear a view this time, I see the white amniotic fluid and again the newborn quickly paddling his tail to the surface, mom in pursuit. The baby looks strong and healthy. My heart swells with love.

Two births! To witness two births together seems very unusual. What a blessing! I begin to suspect that the other three births occurred this morning also. Slowly I am filled with the understanding that these dolphins can choose the time of birth for their young. Five females of Pod C chose to have their births at the same time in the shallow waters of the bay today. In the same way that dolphins regulate their bodies and organs when they dive, and choose every breath they breathe, so they also choose the time and place they want to give birth. I am reminded of the phenomena that adult women often experience when their cycles of menstruation are influenced by other menstruating women in their daily environment, as when women who work together in an office are soon having their periods during the same week. Somehow, like the pendulums of grandfather clocks standing side by side in the same room, the rhythmic cycles fall into resonance with each other. Could this be true of families of dolphins who are known to be aware of Earth and cosmic cycles throughout their life in the ocean? The birth of one catalyzes the births of the others.

The thoughts leave my mind as I watch the perfect little babies swimming happily beneath me. I give thanks for their trust and openness and for my wonderful relationship with these Spinners, a relationship that affords me these incredibly special moments of great joy. The dolphins freely share their precious and much loved children with us. These babies remain very friendly throughout their life. This has resulted in a generation of human-dolphin friendships in this location.

Adult female Spinner dolphins can be recognized by their dorsal fins, which are more falcate, or curved, than the males', and when you look at their underside, you see they have four slits on the lower abdomen — the anus, the vagina and two mammary slits for nursing babies. On many occasions I have seen adult males and females drinking milk from the mammary grooves of a lactating female. Usually the mother's young one is not around or has disappeared. Evidently the rich, nourishing, mucous-like fluid can supplement the diet of adult dolphins as well as babies. On the underside of the males there are two slits. One is the anus and one contains the penis which is retractable, thin and flexible. It moves like a little snake over the female's belly, wiggling from side to side, searching for the vagina. The adult male's dorsal fin is more triangular shaped than the female's and as he becomes older, it may even begin to tip over in a forward direction, bending slightly toward his blowhole. This is one way to determine the maturity of the dolphin. The mature male also has a post anal hump on his underside, forward of his fluke.

Dolphins do not sleep in the way that people do. They are conscious breathers, choosing every breath they take. To do this, they must always be awake. This was learned forty years ago when scientists anesthetized dolphins and were perplexed when the dolphins died. Dolphins need to be awake at all times to breathe. Theirs is an advanced level of evolution that requires being conscious every minute and responsible for the continuation of the breath of life. It is believed that dolphins rest certain lobes of their brains while keeping other sections awake and alert to operate the physical functions of their bodies. They are still conscious, surfacing, breathing and diving, but they do not make audible sounds and do not play. In addition, when they breathe they fill ninety-five percent of their lungs with each breath, as compared to humans who fill about thirty-five percent.

Often people ask me about leadership in the dolphin pods. Among these Spinner pods I have observed no individual leaders. Whenever a dolphin makes a strong move in a specific direction, he or she becomes the leader and the rest of the pod follows. The dolphins seem to share a system of communication that uses group mind and relays information throughout the pod instantaneously. I have named this telepathic communication, Pod Mind.

2

POD  MIND

One day in January, 1990 thirty-five members of Pod A surrounded me and took me into their family. I remember feeling something different about our swim that morning. One moment I was on the outside, the next I was one of them, a member of their pod. I became aware of an energy field that surrounded the dolphins as they swam together. There are similar fields that surround animals in herds on the prairie, sometimes referred to as a "ring of light." All the animals in the herd are aware of its boundaries and will protect its sovereignty. If anyone approaches this invisible field from the outside, the animals become restless and paw the ground, preparing to defend their herd. On this morning I became aware of a ring of light around the dolphins. Suddenly I felt myself included in it as a member of the pod. It felt like a cloud of energy had suddenly ballooned out from them and surrounded me, bringing me into their collective field. I felt as if I were a Spinner dolphin. I was swimming swiftly and weaving and breathing as they did with grace and ease. We were moving as a unit and it felt very safe and natural, like coming home to a familiar place. I surrendered to the experience and began to understand a concept I call "pod mind." We were One. We swam alike, we shared a love for the ocean, our bodies were similar, we were no longer different species, our thoughts merged together, and I became aware of my surroundings through their eyes. This is the meaning of pod mind. My entry into their ring of light was my first introduction to their gentle process of communicating with humans, a fascinating and inspiring method that allowed me to experience the world of the dolphins through their group mind.

Swimming in continuous communication with each other continued over the next months with Pod A. One day I realized how natural pod behavior had become for me. As I swam leisurely with the dolphins, I was totally immersed in the feeling of Oneness. There were dolphins next to me on the surface, there were dolphins beneath me and far below. Their beauty and their spirit surrounded me. On and on we swam together. As we entered a shallow area along the side of a cliff, the water was murky and I became vaguely aware of outcrops of coral and rocks below us. Rather than breaking formation, our entire pod gently swerved to permit the dolphins near the coral to avoid it. Without decreasing our tail strokes or stopping or dispersing, without sounds or signals, we moved as one body, spontaneously and simultaneously.

How did they all know to make that same move at once? And how had I known? I had understood the intention to turn left at the same moment as the rest of the pod and had done so automatically, without thought.

This was the beginning of my awareness of the dolphins' proficiency at group mind and simultaneous action. There is a field of energy, and also a field of intelligence, that is transmitted among the pod instantaneously. They have an astounding awareness of the extremities of their bodies, of every other dolphin and person around them and of their immediate environment. Certainly a life in the element of water, where they are physically caressed by their surroundings, contributes to this sensitivity, as well as a lifetime as a member of a consciously and constantly communicating pod. They travel, feed, play and mate within the unit. They are not as inclined to develop individuality as they are inclined to group living and group empathy. In this way, they can be examples to us of how to live in harmony with each other and our environment, how to cooperate and how to form loving communities. When we experience group mind, we move into a place of integrity where everything is known. There are no hidden agendas. For the pod to follow the thought process of one dolphin requires accepting that each dolphin will make the highest and best choice in any given situation for the entire pod. It requires a high level of trust and altruistic caring. It is based on a reality where mutual love and responsibility for each other are the norm. Being a part of the pod mind was a memorable event for me, revealing the natural communication between my unconscious and that of the dolphins, confirming my feeling that I was a part of the pod as we swam together in a fluid unit.

This new way of being together in the ocean was a daily occurrence for Pod A and me. Getting to know them better with each day, feelings of gratitude and respect filled my heart. I was always humbled by the realization of the responsibility inherent in this experience. Accepted as a part of the pod mind, my thoughts and intentions for the dolphins affected their behavior — and yet my knowledge of the ocean was minuscule compared to theirs. I remain very careful to this day, not to direct them or call them to come to me since I know they would lovingly respond — at what possible risk to themselves? Until I know such things as the ocean currents, temperatures, toxins and hazards as well as they do, it would be irresponsible of me to influence them unnecessarily.

ALTERED STATES

One day as we were swimming together, I began to understand more about our jointly-experienced process of group energy. I was with Pod A dolphins, White Stripe, Sunburst and three others synchronistically and meditatively moving on a cool spring morning in 1990. For two hours they flanked me. If anyone had been watching this interaction from the shore, it would have looked as if the dolphins were swimming side by side, close to each other, with the almost imperceptible tip of my snorkel appearing like a human dorsal fin between them. We swam mostly on the surface, revealing their amiable deference to my human and amateur aquatic abilities. Occasionally we dove together. The six of us would arch down underwater, remain there for a minute, then leisurely float up again, returning to the same close formation as before. As we swam, we maintained eye contact. Dolphins do not blink. Their gaze is very intense. Their eyes looked deeply into mine as we swam together. I felt heartwarming joy from their trust in me, privileged to be in their company, aware of the beauty that surrounded us. Profound peace and gratitude filled my heart. As the time slowly passed, I lost touch with my surroundings. I was immersed in pod consciousness.

My link with the dolphins was suddenly interrupted when a swimmer purposely darted into our path and excitedly waved her hand at me underwater. Her intent was merely to say hello, but the action was so abrupt and startling that it jarred me out of my reflective state. To suddenly see a human face and to feel the disturbance of this friendly yet shocking intrusion made me react involuntarily. I jumped. The dolphins jumped. We all scattered in different directions, the way the Spinners do when something unexpected comes into their path. I wondered if my reaction had startled them, if the swimmer had startled them (or had they been aware of her approach?), or if they had jumped in a physical/vibrational reaction to my behavior and they were not startled at all. In any case, the interaction ceased, the dolphins joined the greater pod, and I swam back to shore. It had been a painful shock to my dreamlike state — and in retrospect, a very helpful occurrence.

Normally after I swim closely with a group of dolphins, my altered state of consciousness diminishes as more swimmers arrive, or boats approach, or the rest of the dolphin pod comes to playfully interact with us. Other times, after a slow swim back to shore, I arrive on land and am reacclimated to the terrestrial world of gravity and physical matter without realizing an altered state has occurred. But the effect of this startling interruption was to make me immediately aware of the shift in my consciousness, and of how deeply the dolphins and I had been immersed in a trancelike state. We had moved into a different dream-space together. It had happened easily, naturally, and I had not realized how engaged we were until I was jolted out of it.

That night I met with a group of fifteen friends for our weekly meditation. As we focused our thoughts and feelings on planetary healing and human kindness, I became aware of the similarity between our meditative group energy and that of the dolphin pods. I understood more than ever the importance of meditation, and the power of our combined thoughtforms to manifest new realities where Love is our mutual resource. I realized the potential of learning from the dolphins about the power of group mind and the significance of the dolphin teachings in relation to what we could do as a pod of humans working together.

January 14, 1990

Swimming slowly out from the beach, wondering if the dolphins are in the Bay today. Every so often I stop swimming for a look around. No sight of them anywhere. I look at their favorite swimming spot along the coraline cliffs, focusing my vision because their dark wet fins are sometimes indistinct against the dark cliff walls. Hardly breathing I remain silent searching the top of the water, listening for the sound of a burst of air from a blowhole. Nothing but the shorebirds, whose sounds deceive me with their similarity to dolphin whistles.

Well, it's a beautiful day and I feel good. So I'll just enjoy a long, leisurely swim. There's a six foot Manta ray, like an angel ahead of me. I change my swim stroke making my arms emulate the ray's gentle flowing wings...feeling like a ray now. It's hardly moving and soon I pass it.

I meet an outrigger canoe with my neighbors in it. They are fishing and ask if I've seen any fish. Matter of fact, I did...a whole school of them back about ten yards, swimming close to the sand. Must have been three hundred of them. I in turn ask them if they've seen any dolphins. My neighbors have lived on the shores of this bay for fifty years and see dolphins often. They've never paid much attention to them. But we have become friends and because of my interest they have begun noticing the dolphins and reporting their whereabouts to me. Now they tell me, "Oh yeah, they're out there. Way out there where the bay flows into the ocean, past the lighthouse." We all look in that direction and see nothing.

Saying good-bye I continue to swim in the general direction they indicated. There are no other swimmers around at this early morning hour and I feel so good in the peaceful clear water. I love stretching my muscles, exaggerating my swim strokes, feeling the pull on my body. I am completely enjoying the gentle rocking of the ocean and the view through my mask of the many schools of colorful fish. I take a moment to look above water again, and this time I see a splash, far out where the headlands extend into the ocean. Holding still, I watch, and sure enough, there it is again. The Spinners are there and they are in a playful mood. I feel so fortunate to be in this place at this time, sharing this crystal clear water with them, experiencing the same joy that they are feeling.

The sun is warm and glistening on the water. I am relaxed and happy. I feel no need to go after them or exert myself to join them. Giving them a sign of recognition, I raise my arm out of the water and drop it unbending, flat against the water's surface, creating a loud splash, like a humpback whale slapping its pectoral fin. Two more times I send this impact vibration into the water before resuming my easy swimming strokes. They are far away and I don't think I'll swim that distance to find them. Instead I continue to enjoy the underwater fish show as I stroke easily through the water, singing now through my snorkel. It feels wonderful today just to be in the same warm waters with them. Singing and singing, I develop a synchronistic movement that complements the melody. Everything is easy and flowing.

Now I see a large fish. Is it a shark? They are often here, but I find them nonthreatening. They keep their distance...actually seem uninterested in me. They often travel alone in this bay. I wonder if they come here when they are injured or old. I've seen them swimming among fish and the fish are not frightened. I often mistake them for dolphins at a distance, before I notice the characteristic shape of their tail and the horizontal weaving pattern of their swimming. This one seems to be very old or ill. As I approach he is hovering silently on the bottom, hardly moving. That's unusual behavior. I don't alter my direction but continue forward, watching and singing.

Then I look again. It's not a shark, it's a dolphin! How odd, a lone dolphin, just moving with the gentle underwater currents. I am happy to see him. He rolls slowly to one side and eyes me. Feeling so in tune with the ocean I continue to sing and swim in time, slowing my song to curiously observe him. Is he awake? Languidly he moves up from the bottom toward me and to my wonder, he surfaces on my left side and begins to swim with me. Momentarily I hold my breath and forget my song while continuing to swim, as I look sideways at his huge, amazing form right beside me. I feel the warmth of his dark eyes observing me trustfully. Now I resume singing my song and gently kicking my legs, leaving my arms at my sides. His eyes are nearly closed as he swims slowly. If I reach out one hand I could touch him. I sense it would not be right to do.

Together we swim in perfect harmony exactly in pace with each other. I have no thoughts of where we are going. I will swim with this new friend for as long as he will accompany me. It feels wonderful. He must be swimming so slowly to match my snail's pace, but he does it...remaining eye to eye with me. On and on we go as I sing the same little song over and over again. He must think this is my signature sound! After a half mile of side by side, my dolphin friend moves ahead, circles around and suddenly returns with two other dolphins. Now where did they come from? He takes his place again on my left side as the other two swim on my right. I am surrounded. Somehow I continue to sing and kick in time. The melody is slow and easy. We all flow with the music. One of the dolphins has lesions all over his flank. They are round holes that are puckered and seem to be healing. As the dolphin on my right moves slightly ahead, I can see the strong muscles on his torso that bulge as they propel his tail easily up and down. His dorsal fin has a curved gash that has healed over.

I sense that the group is slowly navigating a turn to the right, as the dolphin on my left angles toward me allowing me time to slowly turn my body with the others. Feeling safe in their midst I relax even more and become aware of a sensation of expansion, as if my body has grown larger. I am experiencing being part of a larger body, of a whole, as if I were a piece of a greater unit that is moving in unison through the water. No longer am I conscious of my personal body floating in the water, instead I am aware of being inside a larger unit that extends my physical boundaries much further than they previously were. My thoughts blend with the beings next to me in the water and I feel our connection. It is a feeling of family, and it is an experience of an undivided whole. We are not separate beings that have come to-gether to play or dance, we are a whole (a whale!) where each individual feeling and need is understood by the greater consciousness of One and responded to by all of us. I remember the words of the entity Bashar, channeled by Darryl Anka, who once said that a *whale* is actually a group of dolphins who felt so close to each other, that they decided to reincarnate in one body next time round, and so they came back as a whale. That's what we've done today...become a whale.

THE DOLPHINS KNOW US

Have you ever had the feeling that something much bigger than you is controlling your experiences on Earth? There are many dimensions in which we live. In the third dimension, we are often subjected to the beliefs of the collective consciousness of the world population. In fourth-dimensional reality, we take responsibility for everything that happens to us and understand that we orchestrate all the amazing events of our lives. We write our own curriculum for evolution. Then there is also another reality where the process of group mind, or unified field, is acknowledged as a guiding force. We are not separate from it, our vibratory field is a part of the unified field of all life forms and thereby part of the unfolding reality that we witness around us. In this reality the wisdom of our higher selves is guiding us. We are part of the unified field of evolving Love.

I often feel the influence of this unified field around the dolphins. What made me choose the surname Ocean in 1975, when I didn't even know how to swim and would have no interest in cetaceans until nine years later? It certainly seems to imply that a guiding force or guardian angel was directing my life with the dolphins and it was foretold back then, before I even knew it was a possibility. I remain open to learning what the dolphins may already know about me and my vibratory identity. I am always discovering new things about myself and my life as I swim among them.

June 11, 1991

Today I received a message from the energies of the dolphins for all of the human race. They asked that we learn again to connect and communicate with Nature. Not that we just walk or swim through our natural surroundings, but that we open ourselves to fully experience the wisdom of the natural world. They said that in this connection we will find happiness because being in total communication with all the forces of nature that are constantly around us brings us joy.

We are joyful in the ocean. It is not just a part of our personalities, it is because at all times we are in deep conversation with the elements of the ocean that surrounds us. This is what makes us joyful. As we swim and play in the water, we allow the wisdom of the water, of the sand, of the plankton, of the fish, of the coral, of all the life forms to enter our awareness and inspire us.

It is such a harmonic and intelligent transference of information that we are constantly amused and stimulated. It brings forth knowledge from us and so as we play and interact with you, we are immersed in a process of self education with nature, a process of evolutionary expansion. It is not education as you know it. It is an education through mergence...where the experiences of one or many species are transferred into another in a cellular way which is holographic and experiential. It is such fun to play with the memories and feelings of all the life forms in the ocean.

We play with your memories and wisdom also. It is amazing what we pick up from you. Sometimes it is like an amusement park ride...it goes up and down like emotions do. You are a very loving race and yet you have some resistance in your expression of it. We are intrigued by your complexity and we also enjoy bringing forth some of the qualities that your society does not seem to cherish. Qualities such as tenderness, exuberance and playfulness. When we evoke these qualities in you, we can respond in kind with the same ones, and from our interaction, we then magnify and create greater fields of emotions or expressions to play with. These expressions can truly be "played with" because they are vibrations. It is great fun to feel the expressions in the water. If only you were able to feel these you would understand how much fun we have with the very simple yet unknown (by you) process of communicating vibrationally with all of life.

Sometimes you certainly do feel the vibrational world that surrounds you, but often you are too busy or preoccupied to perceive it. Nothing is more meaningful or necessary for continued evolvement on Earth than the cellular, mental and spiritual vibrations that are available to you in your natural environment.

You can easily learn to play with these vibrations. It is helpful if you are mindful of your diet and your relationships with all things. It is an attitude of appreciation and respect that opens you to the communication. Do not clutter your mind with nonessentials, live simply so that you have free time to dream and listen. We are always available to you.

The Loving Energies of Your Dolphin Friends

HEALTH AND HEALING

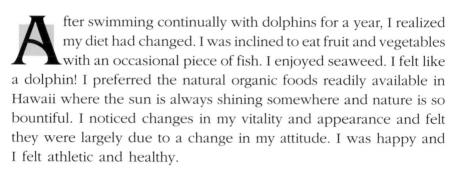

After swimming continually with dolphins for a year, I realized my diet had changed. I was inclined to eat fruit and vegetables with an occasional piece of fish. I enjoyed seaweed. I felt like a dolphin! I preferred the natural organic foods readily available in Hawaii where the sun is always shining somewhere and nature is so bountiful. I noticed changes in my vitality and appearance and felt they were largely due to a change in my attitude. I was happy and I felt athletic and healthy.

Using my muscles and working my body was a new experience for me. As a child I had not been physically active. I liked to sit quietly in my backyard and play among the roots of the old maple and chestnut trees. For hours I made up stories about the elves who lived there, using a few tiny dolls to interact with my elf friends. In public school, I felt apprehensive about physical education and tried to be invisible in the gymnasium. When my classmates were choosing players for baseball games, I felt embarrassed because no one wanted me on their team. It seemed to me I was always the last to be chosen. Eventually I solved that discomfort by becoming very ill with rheumatic fever, an illness of the heart that required a slow convalescence with no athletic activities. I recovered completely when school ended, but consequently, as I matured, I had little awareness of my body's athletic capabilities and my inherent kinship to the earth.

In 1976 I began to explore and enjoy my relationship with nature for the first time when my friend Tysen introduced me to hiking and camping. This was fun and I learned about the beauty of the outdoors and its gifts of renewal. I had always enjoyed walking to shops with my parents when I was a child in New Jersey, and now as an adult on the hiking trails of southern California I learned that my legs were strong. I began a daily exercise program that helped me release many old belief systems and energy blocks about feeling betrayed by my weak body. The tears flowed as I remembered the anger and frustration from my impressionable childhood.

The dolphins seemed to be aware of my generally inactive lifestyle and they provided a regular workout of endurance swims for me. This was especially apparent whenever I returned from a few weeks away from Hawaii. The workouts included my swimming alongside them for many miles and many hours. Only after I had recovered my previous level of endurance in the water would the next lesson begin. Sometimes I felt my heart would burst from the exertion of maintaining their pace, and yet I never wanted to interrupt our adventure because I was having so much fun. This was another lesson I appreciated...make education and exercise fun and you have a willing student!

Soon swimming became easy. I could dive deeper and hold my breath longer while I swam with the dolphins. Making dives in quick succession, I learned how to take short and full breaths in a split second. First spouting fully to empty my snorkel, then rolling over to swim belly up like them, I used my fins to propel me along in a "dolphin swim" style called "mo-tor-boating." I practiced diving and releasing a barrage of bubbles from my snorkel, making a wall of bubbles! Spiraling into the rays of light that danced below, I became a water being.

April 1, 1993

I have just returned from a two-week trip to Japan where I presented eight workshops about our dolphins in Hawaii and visited Mt. Fuji and the Tokyo Aquarium. This morning I jump out of bed with a start because I know without looking that the dolphins have arrived. I wake up my friends from Australia, Inta, Shirley and Anne, to let them know, and then without waiting for even a hot drink, I am in the water. I have missed the dolphins and I know they are here to see me. As soon as I clear the coral rocks through the water passageway from my back yard, I head for mid-bay and begin singing my favorite dolphin song. I haven't completed one verse before the dolphins are upon me, surrounding me in great numbers and swimming alongside me. What joy we all feel. I love you, I tell them. They know, they feel the same about me. On and on we swim together, diving and playing and circling the bay.

My calves and ankles feel weak from lack of exercise while in Japan, but the pod respects my pace and swims slowly with me. They sonar me intensely and I am certain they are immersing themselves in all the new information in my cells from the wonderful interactions I had in Japan with people who care about dolphins. Then they send all their latest news to me, proudly showing me their babies who have grown in my absence. The two young babies who were born in January are now rounder, fuller in the tummy, and there is a new baby, just born yesterday judging from his skinny wrinkled appearance and tiny fluke. He swims closely beneath his mother, not leaving her side. They have been with the humpback whales, and are sending me an acoustic image of the new births, the huge, gentle whale babies; the dolphins imitate their sounds.

This pod of fifty-eight dolphins traveled to the other side of this island while I was away, swimming with new pods of dolphins, having their yearly reunions. Now they are back along the Kona coast and we are all happy. Most of the communication between us is an exchange of feelings of joy and a healing of my body as they sonar it and fill it with energy to replenish what I lost during my days out of the water. We swim for many hours before I return to shore to rest and to remain with their love. I am energized, and aware that with very little sleep and no breakfast, I can still swim tirelessly when in the presence of the pod.

INFINITE ENERGY

This is a revelation shared by many people who swim among dolphins. We do not get tired or hungry or thirsty. Our energy levels are high and inexhaustible. Swimming in close proximity to dolphins boosts our vitality and strength. We also become joyful, laughing and singing as we swim together and watch the clever antics of the dolphins around us.

The dolphins explain that we have reserves of strength within us that we can call on as we wish, to increase our physical potentials. They liken it to the so-called "empty space" in outer space, identified by scientists. Empty space is actually not empty at all, but is a reservoir of infinite energy in the universe. It also exists in the molecules and smallest atomic particles of our bodies. When we feel love or joy, our metabolism changes, and this in turn activates the energy in the space between our cells, making bioelectric reserves of energy available to us. The dolphins are masters at achieving this state of quiet mind and alert body. "Active relaxation" such as this is healthy for our physical and subtle bodies. We are beginning to change because of it. People who swim with wild dolphins every day are infused with a gentle acceptance of the world and its inhabitants. We become peacemakers wherever we are. Our capacity for gratitude and level of contentment increase.

HEALING WITH LOVE

Many people believe that dolphins have the power to heal. However, it's not that dolphins heal people…it's that being with them helps people regain their natural healthy state.

The dolphins have shown me that we need to move beyond our belief in physical, three-dimensional reality. Materialistic reality is an illusion. Instead we live in a universal field of energy that is the source of ALL possibilities. It vibrates, it is alive. It is unmanifest potential and it is a frequency we call Love. When Love lives in the cells of our bodies, everything within its field is created in perfect order. There is no illness. It is not that the illness is cured — it just ceases to exist.

The dolphins have helped me understand that there is a cell-to-cell transmission of a healing vibration that is awakened whenever we are in the presence of Love. It is this energy that heals, not an energy from an external source. It is an ever-present, refined energy, that when consciously shared between receptive individuals has the power to heal. It is always present in our bodies.

Our vibrational forms radiate sound waves that produce health and strength in our physical and energetic systems. When this frequency is disturbed by incompatible thoughtforms such as anger, jealousy, fear, limiting belief systems and negative thinking, fragmentations result. If seen by the eye they would appear as wrinkles, ridges, dents, discolorations, and erratic vibrations in our etheric forms. The resulting systems operate in a less than optimal way, often impacting the body, mind and auric fields with reactions we call disease, depression, anger, stress, separation, sadness and fear.

Most people have had the experience of sadness suddenly being transformed to joy. For example, we may feel alone and depressed when a situation does not work out as we had planned. Then in the same day, someone or something comes along bringing us so much joy that the sad feelings are gone in a twinkling! So how much credence can we give to unhappy feelings? They are fickle and not worth making us sick. If we immerse ourselves in the beauty and joy of life in every moment, we can eliminate negativity.

When the illusion of illness disappears, the intelligence within our cells is there to allow wellness. It can happen instantaneously. We don't need to GET well over time, we can merely accept the perfection of our cells, and we will be well. Fully embracing our true vibrations, Love, Joy and Gratitude, is the quickest way to achieve wholeness and transformation on Earth. This requires omitting everything from our lives that is not Love, and/or redefining and accepting everything in our lives as Love.

Humans are comprised of geometric energy forms, which are in turn connected to greater universal geometric patterns. Within the universal energy systems, we are a perfect part of the whole. If we unknowingly tone down our healthy vibrations, or live in surroundings that alter our vibrations, we will be out of synchrony and contact with the universal vibes. Unlike us, the dolphins are consciously in contact with the Universal metaforms and sigils (complex, evolved universal geometries) at all times.

When we swim among the dolphins our vibratory oscillations are affected by their presence. The pulsating waves of our human and their dolphin life forms come together and are changed by the coupling. People are affected differently depending on their receptivity to dolphins: how long they have been swimming among them, communicating with them, and whether or not they are able to open themselves to the natural healing frequencies the dolphins emit. People's abilities to benefit physically from the dolphins also depends on their relationship to universal energy waves, i.e. their level of awareness with regard to remaining within frequencies of harmony and peace in their daily lives. The dolphins vibrate Love. Love is also the essence of our souls, and it manifests as our cellular matter. Our life experiences impact our cellular matter, sometimes negatively. However, spending time with the dolphins positively affects our brain waves, cardiac electricity, and auric-frequency identification, bringing us into synchronicity with the vibration of Love. The dolphins and whales know how to braid their vibratory wavelength of Love with ours. They are teaching us to play in those waves!

Often people who are healers notice a change in their work after swimming among dolphins. Friends who are massage therapists feel that the dolphins enter their awareness during massage treatments and interact through their hands with the energy fields of their clients. A good example of this is Trish, whose first dolphin encounters with the Spinners included a swim between two dolphins for forty-five minutes. Since then, she has been able to visualize the areas which need healing in the bodies of her Jin Shin Jyutsu clients. The healing love of the dolphins can be transmitted to others through us.

Doug and Trish

My friend Doug remembers the day he saw *Radio*, a dolphin from Pod B, with a large wound on his head. It was a cookie-cutter shark bite that was deep and bleeding. Doug felt great compassion for *Radio* who is always so friendly and playful with us. He said a prayer asking to be a conduit of healing energy. Feelings of love entered Doug's awareness, filling his body with overflowing kindness, and he began to radiate Love. *Radio* was immediately aware of this healing energy and he came directly to Doug. For thirty minutes he stayed at Doug's side receiving the healing benefit of his loving intentions — no physical contact was necessary. We noticed that *Radio* healed very quickly after this encounter. When a healing experience like this takes place, the human and the dolphin always have a close bond from that time on. Their fields have been intertwined and they both are enriched by the experience.

December 5, 1993

This morning the dolphins weren't in the bay when I awoke at 7:00. I felt rather groggy because my Hawaiian neighbors had a party down the street with a live band last night. It was great and I loved hearing the families singing with the music. People took turns getting up on the little stage in the park singing through a microphone. As usual it continued all night and I didn't sleep much. I had that heavy, cotton-in-my-head feeling when I woke up! Since the dolphins were not here, I made some hot tea and was soon busily working on my computer. When some children came through my yard, talking about the dolphins, I picked up my binoculars to look at the ocean. Sure enough, there they were playfully splashing on the surface. I wondered which group it would be as I quickly put on my bathing suit.

I swam leisurely out to our meeting place, singing a song. I felt certain it was not Pod A because they would have come to greet me by now, and then after waiting a while longer I decided it was probably not Pod B either. It was 8:30 a.m. and I looked around at the beauty of the water as the sun began to warm me from behind the morning clouds. Suddenly I was surrounded by thirty-eight dolphins. Now where had they come from?

Immediately three large adults swam over, *Tippy, Two Nicks* and *Queen* from Pod C. I was very happy to see *Tippy*. He hadn't been around for five months. It's uncanny how often a particular dolphin appears right after I ask my friends if they've seen him lately. Just yesterday I took a poll of the other swimmers at my house to see if anyone had seen *Tippy*, in case I had missed him in the water. No one had seen him. We all expressed concern for his well-being. Now today he showed up as if to say, "Here I am, I'm fine!"

It was good to swim with him again. His dorsal fin tips to the left and has a little piece missing from the bottom which makes the remaining part stand upright like a pyramid. I knew him when he first joined the pod. He swam by himself for a long time. It was notable because the pod reacted differently to him. It appeared that the other dolphins did not accept him, because they chased him away, a behavior rarely seen among these Spinner pods. He continued to swim on the periphery, and he was eventually permitted to join the pod. I always felt compassion for him and often swam alone with him during those early days. Now I expressed my joy to see him and said a big Hello. He tends to swim a little in front of me, curving his neck to look back and see me with his right eye. It's a wonder he doesn't bump into anything!

Later, as I swam with *Queen*, I realized it was the anniversary of the day I had met her in 1990. The circumstances were unlike anything I've ever witnessed before or since. A large, sixty foot, white yacht with the word "King" in its name came into the bay very fast. There was a woman standing at the bow, pointing at the dolphins and screaming joyfully. The captain steered the boat wherever she pointed. The dolphins tried to move out of the way as the boat careened toward them. Probably to protect me from being run over, since I was in their midst, the dolphins changed course and the boat followed them.

Suddenly a dolphin was hit by the propeller of the boat. I felt sick to my stomach as I saw the confused dolphin swim past me with a look of pain and fear in his eyes. A huge gouge of flesh was missing from his backbone, cut deeply into his back. It was streaming blood and pieces of muscle and skin. Waves from the boat were rocking me wildly from side to side, dolphins were dashing in every direction, the woman was laughing and squealing, the boat was driving erratically. I felt sick from the pain in my heart. How could people be so careless? Dolphins love to ride the bow waves of boats, and they often leave their playtime with me to do this. The boats that frequent the bay are mostly respectful and careful with the dolphins. But this was a new boat. When dolphins ride the bow wave it's important to drive with care and move in the same direction as the pod. Just because you can see some of the dolphins riding the bow wave doesn't mean you should forget that the rest of the pod may be swimming in formation underneath the boat. Evidently no one had advised this boat captain about correct dolphin/boating procedures. I was shocked and in pain for the dolphin.

What could I do? The dolphin, one that I did not yet know, quickly swam away with the rest of the pod. They would take care of him. I didn't see them again that day. In my log notes, I recorded the incident and as I drew a picture of the dolphin who had been the victim, I gave him the name of *King,* to remind myself he was the one hit by the boat named "King."

Day after day I looked for *King* among all the pods. I was so saddened by the memory of his face, first gentle and joyful, then filled with shock and pain. Nearly a year passed, as I continued to look for him. I assumed he had died. Then one day, October 21,1991, he appeared, swimming with Pod C! You can imagine how happy I was. He seemed fine and healthy. The deep wound on his back was still there but the skin had healed over it. I was amazed. I sent him great love and happiness and expressed my joy to see him.

The dolphins were all mating at that time of year and that was how I learned that *King* was actually a female, and so I changed her name to *Queen.* She is beautiful and swims as fast as the others. They have healed her, she has healed herself, the ocean has healed her. I always feel great love for her.

So here she was today swimming with me. My old friend...with no anger toward human beings. Watching me tenderly as she wove back and forth in front and beneath me. Gently brushing her dorsal fin against my stomach as she glided by.

PSYCHOLOGICAL OSMOSIS

Often people ask how they can do the work I am doing. Of course the answer is to learn where the dolphins and whales live and respectfully pay them a visit. Spend as much time as possible in their environment, learning from them. Young people are interested in what courses to take at the university. My degrees are in counseling psychology, and that knowledge has served me well. Empathy and telepathy, skills that effective counselors use, are also important aspects of successful dolphin communication. The compassionate ability to be sensitive to others, to feel what they are feeling, is a quality inherent in all of us. As a therapist, when I experience empathy, clients' feelings enter my entire body and I can feel the pain or joy of people emotionally and physically as they do. I can be moved to tears or laughter by the depth of their pain or happiness.

I then examine the feelings internally and if a problem relates to emotional turmoil, I look at how this problem can be solved as if it were my own. I believe all problems can be solved to the satisfaction of the client who is suffering from them. I determine how to make the pain or anger, which we now share, be transmuted into the Light and into a positive solution.

When I see the Light of this situation and I "feel" the solution within me, the client then receives the healing, the new ideas, the answers directly from me, on more than the intellectual level. The information is conveyed to clients differently depending on their mode of receiving and accepting information, i.e. are they most receptive to rationalizations? To energy healing? To physical touch such as massage or reflexology? To spiritual understandings that take them beyond the narrow view of third-dimensional reality? Or is their solution found in the discovery of a support system among people and nature that they may have overlooked? Sometimes people's basic problem is a grieving for their separation from nature, although they may not identify it as this initially. As I feel the resolution of the problem and the pain lessening in my psyche and body, clients feel it in their own bodies as well.

To empathize effectively it is important to first clear our own emotional issues. Sometimes people ask me why their lives are not unfolding in the way they wish. There are reasons for these snags in the process. If your spiritual power is being diluted by numerous unresolved emotional ties and beliefs, you may not have enough pure, high-frequency energy available to radiate a clear energetic image of your needs. If your plans require the support financially, emotionally or intellectually of other people, those people's attitudes toward your ideas can affect the manifestation. If your plans are based on ego needs, glamour and temporal gratification, they may only be fulfilled through the timeworn methods of struggle and hard work. Ego-centered desires are part of the old paradigm and the new energies of Earth no longer support that method of evolvement. But, if your dreams and goals are humanitarian and align with your spiritual purposes for being on Earth, the forces of universal love will ensure their attainment. Whenever we are still attached emotionally to past events in our lives, we are draining away our internal life force, diminishing our abilities to help others.

It might be helpful to get a pen and pad right now and see where your energy is going. List all the people and occurrences about which you have an emotional charge, going all the way back to your childhood. Then close your eyes and feel or see whether these emotional issues are attached by cords which drain your energy. If so, this is where your power is going. Ask for spiritual assistance and then release the emotions into the Light. Don't worry. If they are people or things that are meant to remain in your life, they will. But they will now be strong and healthy relationships rather than co-dependent ones.

Swimming with dolphins can also help us identify these energy drains in our lives. When the dolphins swim alongside us, their loving presence puts us in touch with deep feelings. We can no longer hide the parts of ourselves that are in dissonance with the natural health and harmony of our bodies and emotions. The dolphins are carriers of Light, and in their presence all that is not Light becomes tenderly exposed so that it can be examined with clarity and sensitivity. It feels as though all their unconditional love washes over our fears, doubts and temporal concerns and returns us to a pure awareness of our true identities as powerful Light beings who live by the simple task of giving and receiving Love and Joy. Dolphins know that feelings other than Love are merely three-dimensional emotional thoughts that are limiting and depressing. Once we understand these feelings as such, we can realize they are merely part of our human incarnation on Earth and not part of the essence of our souls, and we can joyfully release them in order to return to harmony again. With this new knowledge, we find we are uplifted, we suddenly have solutions, we are creative and optimistic.

This is what happened to me during my first communication with a California Gray whale as described in my book, *Dolphin Connection: Interdimensional Ways of Living*. At that time, before I had met any dolphins, the whale shared an energy force with me that entered my body and auric field and changed my feelings of depression to feelings of well-being (*whale being*). Although I had no previous awareness of the magnificence of the sea and its essential part in preserving the Earth, my mind filled with an understanding of the whale's love of the ocean. Suddenly, I loved the ocean and wanted to help the planet. I wanted to know the ocean and swim in it. Why did I feel this way? The whale had transformed my feelings by merging his wisdom with mine. I felt it physically in my body as a deep state of peace. I felt huge waves of Love melting my separateness. A deep love of our Earthly home is the normal vibration for whales, and because my heart had been open, I had been able to receive the vibration and let it activate my own powerful essence. The whale's gift was to show me an effective method of healing. To be able to do it, you need to feel love for the person or animal or plant or entity with whom you are merging. Love is the wavelength that stimulates the interaction, communication and healing.

In Hawaii, my friends and I are learning to experience the empowering energy of the dolphins' loving world. Swimming together, we create a feeling of harmony similar to that achieved in deep meditation. Our senses are amplified. Any subtle motions we make are felt by each of us. In this actively meditative state, we hear sounds over long distances, our bodies are propelled forward on the dolphins' water flow fields, we swim synchronistically and our energy fields merge. Individual boundaries are suspended, and we move in rhythm with each other's heartbeats. This energy merge is a vibrational communication that nurtures intimacy between our species — and is preparing us for contacting other realms and meeting the beings there.

Because of this intimacy I have come to realize the dolphins can read my energy field clearly and far beyond the capacity of our present technology and understanding. They can perceive my feelings about them, the gladness in my heart, the condition of my body, my feelings of safety with them, my appreciation of their beauty, the trivia on my mind, the depth of my being as I stare unembarrassed into their eyes, my gratitude and love. It is all there and I feel our alignment with each other, species to species. They reflect the beauty and intelligence of my own consciousness and thereby allow me to see myself in a new way. Our swims infuse me with their ancient knowledge, leave me wondering what else in the world is more significant, more profound, than our deep connection to our oceans and earth, the mutual cycles of growth, the spirals of life that exist in all animate forms, and the recognition of our historical, universal and spiritual bonds.

LEARNING TO SPIRAL

June 27, 1992

The dolphins arrive a little late today at 7:15. I have a cup of tea and am in the water by 7:30 a.m. The bay is empty on this gray morning, a feeling of rain in the air. The water is warm and calm. I swim leisurely. My old fins have a tear in them and I notice how they impair my swimming today. I see my neighbor, Chuck, on his boat — no one else. The dolphins are invisible. I swim toward the cliff where three pyramid-like shapes in the rocks are outlined on the pali cliff, and wait. Now I see fins coming toward me. How many are there? I only see five or six. Suddenly *Peduncle Dash* is upon me. He quickly circles me very closely and looks in my eye. I am happy to see him and we immediately swim side by side. My dorsal fin/snorkel tube cuts the water next to his.

Soon *Scratches* and *Crater* join us and the four of us weave and swim close together. My heart is filled with such joy in their presence! They stare at me and look deeply into my mask as they turn to swim beneath or in front of me. My morning is complete. My friends have come to meet me, they have welcomed me joyously, and they stay with me now, ignoring the rest of the pod which swims demurely along the sand beneath us. On and on we go together.

Demonstrating their different personalities, *Scratches*, *Crater* and now *Wave* swim serenely, grandly next to me while *Peduncle Dash* is very excited. He weaves in and out among us, nearly colliding with me, but of course never quite doing so. Such precision, such exuberance! Now he is chattering and swimming in front of us, rapidly nodding his head. As usual, he becomes so excited he hurls himself out of the water. I look up and laugh as I watch him flying through the air as though someone is casually tossing him up out of the water. Over and over again he leaps, what appear to be aimless jumps, and yet he makes a perfect circle around *Scratches, Crater, Wave* and me. Soon he has completed a dozen twisting jumps and he resumes his place by my side, nosing his way among the others, gazing at me expectantly, sensing my approval and love.

We continue swimming side by side, but I can feel *Peduncle Dash's* excitement rising. After five minutes he zips away again and heads for the sky! Many aerial spins in a row. I love watching him both above water and below, as he crashes down from the sky and sinks beneath the surface in a cloud of fizz and bubbles. He straightens his body, powers his flukes into action, and propels himself out of the ocean again. Sometimes *Scratches* joins him in his leaps, and they fly out of the water in perfect synergy, even the same body angles, like identical twins. They spin in the air repeatedly, surrounding me with a circle of leaps. I am immersed in tickling white foam and bouncing rainbow bubbles. Now other dolphins from the larger pod join them in the air and suddenly the bay is filled with exuberant, joyful dolphins jumping every which way!

BEING A DOLPHIN

As interest in dolphins grew internationally, more people were drawn to be with dolphins and some of them found homes to rent near me. With our common interests, six to eight of us swam together daily, noting the behaviors of the different dolphins and sharing the identification and experiences of the pods. The dolphins were encouraging this interaction between themselves and our human pod, and they developed more intriguing behaviors to entice and entertain us.

I soon realized that more was occurring than mornings of simple play and exercise. The dolphins were determined to teach those of us who were interested how to appreciate and understand the ocean and its special inhabitants. Our role was to watch, listen and mimic their pod behavior. In this way, we would learn. The dolphins wanted to pass on their intelligence to us if we could grasp the meaning of their communications. It was up to us to transcend the limitations of our human programming and open ourselves to these new possibilities.

Some of their teachings rely on the natural tendency of people to mimic behavior, like children mimic the behavior of adults. The dolphins swim so fluidly through the water. We try to do likewise, but often feel clumsy in their presence. Our fins rub against each other, our masks fill with water, we sputter and flap! We dive with great effort and return to the surface quickly, seeking air. The dolphins inspire us to be more fluid and graceful in the water and on the land.

The Spinners are Light dancers! They fly into the air and spin and twist. Watching them, I feel such a strong urge to do likewise. I wish I could propel myself out of the water and spin in midair, watching the world of brown cliffs, green trees and colorful rooftops whiz by me in a kaleidoscope of dizzying impressions. It must be an amazing experience. Sometimes in the spirit of fun, I kick my fins hard and try to propel myself straight up out of the water, stretching my neck as if it could lift me into the sky. I don't get very far, and yet I sense they are trying to show me something important.

AS ABOVE, SO BELOW

One day I was curiously watching the dolphins Line and Crater poised upside down in the water. It was unusual to see them suspended in this inverted position. Then Wave joined them, floating head down, and began to spiral while in that position. The dolphins and I had been playing a game called "Can You Do This?" in which we mimic each other. It was my turn to copy their behavior. I dove underwater and then, vertically, with my head down, my arms flat against my sides and my legs above me, I began to use the power of my legs to rotate in a spin. It was actually quite easy, spiraling fast in one place. Feeling dizzy and disoriented when I stopped, I kicked to the surface to take a breath.

Where were the dolphins? My upside-down spinning had made me lose my bearings. As I searched the blue depths beneath me with my eyes, I suddenly received a message: *"As above, so below."* And with that communication came an image of the dolphins doing their aerial spins above water. *"As above, so below."* Ah! I've got it! Like a flash of light, the meaning of the message became clear. What the Spinners could do so acrobatically above water in the air, I could do beneath the water's surface. They are water beings who spin in the air; I am an air being who can spin in the water. Of course! I dove, picked up speed and began to spiral very fast under water using my legs to propel me in a vertical spin. How excited I became as I grasped the significance of this communication.

My mind filled with wonder and clarity as the entire dolphin pod swam into view. I dove down again and repeated the spinning exercise, the dolphins all around me chattering noisily, expressing their excitement that I had understood their message. As they circled me, they encouraged my spinning dive and seemed to be commending my efforts. I couldn't wait to do it again, to try it over and over, to perfect the technique, to experience the altered awareness and even physical changes that might occur from the practice of this dolphin behavior.

After I learned to spiral fast underwater, I noticed the dolphins doing this in pairs. So another swimmer and I practiced diving beneath the water, facing each other and placing our snorkel masks against each other. Without touching, we would maintain eye contact and begin to fluke together in synchronistic strokes. We found that we could move quickly, swimming and spiraling parallel to the ocean floor, remaining underwater longer than usual. It is especially beautiful when couples do this.

I often see a group of eight to twelve dolphins diving and spiraling together. As the sun shines on the water, it creates multiple shimmering rays of light that are wide-set at the surface, and then come together at a point somewhere in the deep blue below. The rays of light spiral and weave, dancing among themselves. The dolphins dive into them in close spinning formation — they look like a flower in slow-motion unfolding. As they spiral down deep, I can no longer see them — only the wobbling rays of light remain as their tails disappear into the depths. I float above, watching and waiting, wondering what has happened to them. Many minutes pass before I see movement, and then the same dolphins return, now rostrum first, spiraling up to the surface. The water is about 120 feet there — where do they go that takes them so long to return? Sometimes I impulsively dive into their midst and travel down with them, wanting to go into the depths of the ocean and beyond, braiding myself smoothly among their descending shapes. They include me as they gracefully spiral in a light stream. But eventually I need to surface for air, and leave them to continue spiraling down into the darkness of the deep blue unknown.

Spinning techniques are useful for accelerating our brain's capabilities. Spinning energizes the circuitry between the hemispheres of our brains which stimulate brain cells. It makes the spiraling forces of nature more accessible to us. In addition, it stimulates the natural spinning propensities of the chakras and energy systems of our bodies, and connects us to other spiraling, universal, geometric wavelengths. Sufi dancers know about this connection and practice accessing alternative realities through their dancing, as do children who seem to naturally love spinning round and round in the playground until they fall on the ground, watching the world magically turn on its own.

There are other important reasons for practicing the spiral. We can create fields of energy for transporting ourselves (our cells) to other dimensions where we can experience additional expansions of our minds. It is important to practice spinning until we can do it with ease. In the water where we are weightless, we can experiment with various techniques to determine which feels most interesting and energizing for us. Spinning in the water amplifies mind expansion, since water serves as a supra-conductor of bioelectric frequencies.

Many people are aware of the use of sacred geometric shapes as etheric vehicles for shifting our realities. We can imagine tetrahedrons and dodecahedrons around us, and access the spin of a golden spiral to merge with the vibration of universal unity. Dolphins do this in the water. It is a powerful habitat. Water is eight hundred times more dense than air. It is a conduit for bioacoustic waves and in the presence of the dolphins those waves are the frequency of Love. We experience the electrification of our cells and the acceleration of our biorhythms. No wonder our hearts are so deeply touched when we swim in the ocean with dolphins and whales. They're singing and spinning on the wavelengths called Love.

October 26, 1994

First day out after the wonderful Workshop in Egypt. I see the dolphins when they awake me at 6:32 a.m. I am excited and anxious to get out in the water, although a moment ago I felt jet-lagged and tired. Now I am hurrying around. I feed Lemuria, my cat, drink a cup of water, put defog on my mask, pull on my bodysuit to ward off jellyfish, grab my fins out of my unpacked suitcase, and head out to the backyard. "I'm on my way. I have missed you and I have so many new stories to share with you this morning." Will they be interactive? No need to ask. I can *feel* that they will be. They are as excited to reunite with me as I am with them.

Out in the bay, I feel their sonar on my body. They are learning everything I experienced in Egypt — the pyramids, the Sphinx, the people and the bottlenose dolphins of the Red Sea. I open my auric field to their gentle probing. Their consciousness merges with mine and I transcend to a space of Peace and Love.

Now I see them, a huge pod swimming thickly around and beneath me. Automatically, I begin to count — I reach seventy-five. They are swimming fast and they are jubilant! I feel their happiness to see me and their joy of swimming. Suddenly energized and strong, I kick into high gear, effortlessly maintaining an even pace with them. They're traveling fast and I watch them pass beneath me. It's okay. This is a normal pattern. Slowing down, I continue in the same direction, letting them move ahead, out of sight. The water is very murky today. There have been high waves in my absence and the dolphins have not been here much. Soon I cannot see any of the seventy-five, even the white bellies of the slowly spiraling dolphins have disappeared into the blue. The sun is about to rise over the eastern mountain and the surface of the water is white. I look up, momentarily wondering in my enthusiasm where they have gone. So humanly impatient for our encounter to continue. I don't have to wait long. Looking down again, ten dolphins are around me, surfacing so close. "Hello my friends, I have missed you." Looking into my eyes, one by one they take turns pushing each other away to make contact. The love I feel for them surges up into my heart and my emotions. I feel my aura expand to twice its size! Love overflowing.

I dive. Three dolphins and I surface together and spout in unison. Now they herd me, swim this way, turn to the left, keep turning in a circle. Round and round I go in a tight circle with *Candle,* a friendly Pod B dolphin. I can tell he thinks it is funny. He turns with ease, while I madly kick one leg in an effort to circle with him, using my other leg as a rudder and not using my arms. Arm movements seem to startle the dolphins and keep them at a distance, so I've learned to strengthen my legs and turn with one fin paddling! A slight cramp threatens the instep of my right foot, but I ignore it. Nothing is more important than maintaining unbroken eye contact with this funny dolphin who chooses to play with me in this remarkable way.

By playing this game, *Candle* keeps me all to himself. There is no room for any other dolphin to slide inside our little circle. Round and round we go. I am upright in the water, turning in place, fifteen and twenty times. This happens repeatedly as now different dolphins take turns interacting with me in this same way. I am glad when *Whitey* changes direction to circle right so I can use my other leg for a while. No matter how long we do this I do not falter. I push myself to keep up with him and stay right at his side, maintaining eye contact. He is on the outside, I am inside. He turns so fluidly, but I jerk along!

I fleetingly wonder what purpose this game serves. Does it exercise certain muscles that I need to improve, does it strengthen my focus on the dolphins, does it distract me while information is being communicated into my cells? Is there no purpose except to play? I really don't care. I act on intuition and it tells me to follow their lead and swim as much like a dolphin as possible. Then I receive an answer... *"This whirling and turning that we are experiencing...we are helping you purify your aura and energy systems by spiraling with you. We are in a spinning star tetrahedron where we enter other spaces."* The dolphins escort me in this adventure! It is being shown to me in the way it is meant to be experienced — as fun, as play. The love I feel has become a spiritual dance sounding my body with joy and activating spiraling, universal wavelengths!

WAVELENGTHS OF LOVE

When our hearts are filled with Love, we radiate a pulse that is capable of producing health and balance in our bodies, energizing us and nurturing longevity. We have control over this pulse and can increase our conscious awareness of it by resonating our brain waves in sync with the low-frequency range of our heartbeats. Studies by Dan Winter (*Alphabet of the Heart; Sacred Geometry: The Genesis in Principle of Language and Feeling*, from Crystal Hill Farm, 9411 Sandrock Road, Eden, New York 14057; telephone: 716-992-9307) have shown that it is possible to consciously affect the frequency of our own hearts. When they pulsate with Love, our hearts can affect our brain waves and the genetic code in our cells, producing boundless energy, good health and proficient mastery of our minds. As Dan relates, "When our space brothers from Sirius tell us that LOVE is the only emotion which is transportable across galactic spaces, we can now understand why. It is the key in the lock to biology's export of memory/program for lifting mass to light . . ." When our loving hearts resonate with our brain waves, we are sending our communication signals to other dimensions. And the wave that traverses dimensions is the one called Love.

This is what the dolphins have been teaching us. By swimming among us, emanating the transformative vibrations of Love, the dolphins have helped us open to the knowledge of this great potential that lives within us. We can experience transformative Love when we are with the dolphins — but we can also learn to access it at any time, and to live within those vibrations on a daily basis wherever we are.

A DREAM

I recall a particular day in 1992 when I did not feel filled with Love. I had some doubts about the usefulness of my work with the dolphins. I wondered if I was really using my skills and contributing to planetary consciousness by swimming among dolphins every day. Would this work really make a difference? Was it the best use of my talents? After all, I had been trained as a Psychologist — perhaps I should be counseling people as I had done previously. That evening, after a day with many emotional upheavals, I asked myself these questions.

Upon going to sleep, I had an extraordinary dream that seemed to last all night. In my dream I felt the gentle communication of legions of Celestial Beings. They were reflecting back to me the Love I have felt for other people during many heartwarming encounters in my lifetime. I was shown a procession of all the people I have loved and cared about, even in small ways, since I was a child. Each person, child and animal walked gently by, looking at me and smiling. I was overwhelmed by the magnitude of love they were sending to me and I awoke from the dream in tears, infused with a great sense of peace.

Immediately I grasped the message…that the love we share and feel for others is amplified into huge waves of loving vibrations that ripple out to affect much more than merely the individual people, animals and nature spirits that we meet. The power of love and caring, when expressed with integrity from the heart, connects with a universal field of Light which sends immense waves of loving energy to our planet and beyond. It is not a matter of *how many* people we express love to, it is the spiritual depth of the feelings of love we express during our daily lives. When the feelings are deeply and purely experienced in our own bodies and minds, the waves of love radiating from us will affect the world. The unified field of Love is then automatically accessed and amplified to resonate compatibly with our own. The dolphins, for example, evoke so much love from swimmers that they provide a wonderful service just by being who they are. This is an ongoing message from the dolphins: *"Be fully who you are. You are a Being of Love."* It's a good reminder for us. The Love that people and dolphins feel when they are together goes out into the world and fills the planet with Love's harmonic vibrations. It transforms people, it transforms the Earth.

This is the importance of communication and interactions with the dolphins. My fleeting doubts about this spiritual work were dissolved in the understanding of humanity's role as Universal Beings of Love.

BRING PEOPLE TO SWIM
WITH US

ach day as I swim into the bay, I sing a song through my
snorkel. It is a familiar melody which happens to have a nice
cadence for kicking my feet in a continuous rhythm, making
it easy for me to swim for many hours. The melody is the popular
American song, "You Are My Sunshine." But I have changed the words
to the following:

You are my dolphins, my lovely dolphins.
You make me happy in every way,
You'll always know dear,
How much I love you,
So come join us, to jump, swim and play!

Since I sing this every day, perhaps you could say it is my "signature
song"...a sound by which the dolphins can recognize me. The
dolphins of Pod A do seem to respond to it by swimming to me,
although it is unclear if they are responding to the sounds or to the
feelings of happiness in my heart when I sing and swim in the ocean.
After a few years I began to notice that the dolphins had learned this
song and were singing it to me! Although they were using their own
language of vocalizations, I could recognize the melody and the tonal
words.

March 31, 1990

Swimming with the dolphins today, I feel so much love. They swim to meet me, responding to my signature song. They are deep beneath me, swimming gracefully. I watch them as I swim above, imitating their undulations. I gaze with appreciation at their familiar forms, at their synchronistic movements, each member moving separately, yet each a part of the whole. As a unit they flow beneath me, aware of me although no one looks up. I swim with a constant and steady beat, merging with the spherical field of the pod. I am with them, fifty feet above them. Yet soon, even as I swim strongly and quietly, they are moving ahead. All I can see are their flukes as they swim into the blueness. I feel a loss that my vision does not extend further.

Now all is silent. I stop breathing to hear them. No sounds of sonar fill the waters today, no burst of breath as they surface. Stillness.

Quietly I move my fins, my arms are motionless at my sides. I am content. I have seen them, I have participated in their circle if only for a moment.

Lifting my head from the water, I use my eyes to search the surface...waiting patiently to see past the whitecaps that obstruct my view. There! I think I see them over by the cliff! There are the black fins on the surface, cutting through the water and coming in my direction. My heart fills with a song of welcome.

Thirty-five dolphins come back to see me, to include me in the closed circle of their pod. All around me now, tilting their heads to gaze at me, whistling their sounds at me, checking my body, balancing its energy fields. On the surface we swim together. We spout together, exhale, inhale. Then one dolphin dives, and the next one, and the next...following each other down into the depths of the ocean. Fascinated by the beauty of their movements, I am the last to dive, trailing behind. So deep they go while I dive half as far and then return to the surface for air. Slowly they turn and swim upward towards me. Right beneath me, it looks as though they will surface in the very spot where I am swimming. Needlessly I fluke hard to move out of their way. I feel responsible in my love for them, to cause them no harm, to never inconvenience them. With an imperceptible motion they glide to the right and the left of me, looking into my eyes and reassuring me that my presence is a blessing. Returning to the surface one by one and in groups of four or five, they spout; and we begin again to swim together, side by side on the surface.

Below I see the mothers and nursing babies. The babies are curious. They break away from their mothers, the older ones first, coming close in the water to sonar me. I wonder if the mothers and aunties will be concerned about their babies, but I receive no indication of this. The adults in the pod watch, but no one stops the youngsters from coming to see me. A quick look, and the young ones are back at their mothers' sides, nursing and swimming in their water flow-fields.

On and on we go, swimming side by side, diving, pivoting, changing direction. My body feels so bulky sometimes as they gracefully turn below me and I paddle and kick to turn and stay with them. Do they find me funny? I laugh aloud, picking up their feelings and communications. Dolphins are funny! People are funny! Life is an experience of joy and laughter.

Now swimming together for hours...I ask them, how can I help? How can I give as much love as they do? How can I spread their Light? Is there anything I can do to help them?

An immediate answer:

"Swim with us and bring people to swim with us."

I feel this answer from within. I know this is correct. Though there may be times when I doubt it — am I disturbing them? Am I changing their behavior? Is it better if they don't befriend humans? I don't want to do anything that would hurt them, not ever. But these are human fears and human concerns. They are not the thoughts of the dolphins. The dolphins are overjoyed to meet new and interesting people. This is a great interspecies reunion. What fun to be a part of it!

October 21, 1991

Line moved to my left and we swam eye to eye. This seemed very significant, as if a longlasting friendship was being honored. Together we would bend and dive shallowly, roll and swim belly to belly, returning together to the surface. Sometimes we made complete circles underwater two times before surfacing. I found I could easily hold my breath, and that diving was effortless. It was trancelike, yet at the same time I felt alert and capable of great strength and endurance. We continued to swim for three hours without stopping.

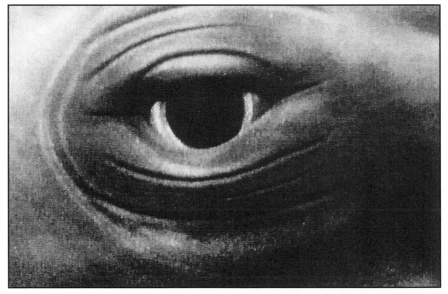

Zari Productions ©

Somehow our eye contact during this experience was mind-altering. I cannot lose the feeling and the image of *Line*'s eye looking directly into mine, at the exact same level as my own eye. What did I see? I saw his soft brown eye with a shining black pupil. I saw many small wrinkles around his eye, and scratches above and below that were superficial and looked like teeth marks. The surrounding skin looked very white next to the darkness of his brown eye. I felt an amazing sense of awareness and depth of all-knowing intelligence that is beyond my ability to describe. I was immersed in an angelic love that felt both healing and playful!

His eyes conveyed a sense of seriousness, as though a message was being communicated that was not to be taken lightly. Since dolphins do not blink, it is very powerful when they look at me steadily without breaking their gaze. It is as if they transmit information to me through our eye contact, bypassing the rational and going directly into — where? Into my inner knowing, into my essence. Into the information "transistors" in my cells. And what did I get from *Line?* What did I learn? I felt love, I felt certainty about my work, about continuing to swim with dolphins regardless of the barriers the physical world may throw up. I felt the importance of people swimming with dolphins. I felt the core of myself, an entity with no limitations. I felt as if I could understand, know, do all things in that nurturing space *Line* and I co-created. If I had any questions, any problems, any illnesses, I could work them out. I was in touch with the Mana (a Polynesian term meaning life force) — it was in me, and this contact with *Line*'s eye and my proximity to his vibrational wisdom made its power accessible to me. I became One with Universal Love.

EVOLUTION OF CONSCIOUSNESS

Since 1984 I have been bringing people and wild dolphins together to learn about love and joy from each other, and to experience the power of group intentions. Most of the people who join my Seminars are ready for major life changes and are pioneers in developing advanced human potentials. They have a strong foundation of faith in the ultimate good of the Universal plan and they realize that peace on this planet begins with themselves. They are sensitive, aware men and women who represent the prototype for the new human. They are the way-showers for those people who are searching for more fulfilling lifestyles in careers and relationships.

In the past, evolutionary processes on this planet were evidenced by mental and physical changes. Now we have reached a new plateau in our evolution that requires more than the change of our physical form. It requires a major shift in consciousness. This new consciousness comes from within us. It propels us beyond our present capabilities. With it we access information beyond what we've learned in our schooling, our culture and with our five senses. Along with the dolphins, there are people already living with this new awareness. They are available to teach us when we are ready to explore the possibilities. It is an inspiring and exciting time in our evolutionary unfoldment.

We are learning how to merge with our environment in a way that creates health in our bodies, strength in our minds, compassion in our emotions and grace in our spiritual lives. It results in our manifesting whatever we choose, provided our purposes are in harmony with the divine plan of the greater universe. It brings us daily peace of mind and feelings of great love for all life forms. We participate in the circular exchange of sustaining love, giving and receiving as part of the whole. It is natural and simple. We realize that a key to this new consciousness involves releasing our attachments to all the materialistic and emotional obstacles of our past so that we can more fully experience the reality of Love in every aspect of our lives.

LIVING IN MULTIPLE DIMENSIONS

There are many different realities existing simultaneously all around us. All beings, whether from this planet or another, have their own view of reality. If you are ready to experiment with adventuring into other realities, we can begin to understand the process together. In the past we accepted certain belief systems and then through our vibrational frequencies, thoughts and actions, we created those beliefs in our lives. For example, we believe it is important to express our feelings, face our fears and overcome them. We may believe something is wrong with us if we cannot meditate, channel, make money, remain in good health, find a love relationship, or identify our spiritual purposes for this lifetime. The list goes on and on. We all have specific personal beliefs about ourselves, as well as ones we have accepted from society. These beliefs are so ingrained and so powerful that we usually feel badly if we cannot live up to them.

Many of us are now discarding "society's norms" and living our lives in new ways. We are following our hearts and asking ourselves what is truly best for our lives, our bodies and our spiritual goals. We feel good taking control of our choices. This is important to do. Some New Age teachings have served their purpose and are ready to be discarded now. The spiritual tools we used to evolve over the last decade were based on third-dimensional reality which is quickly becoming obsolete.

If we are interested in enlightenment, we need to move ahead and away from limited ways of thinking and being. Perhaps we are aware of fears and doubts that we need to overcome. In doing this, remember that in the third-dimensional world it is healthy to have some fears and doubts in order to be alert to physical danger and to question the old paradigms of what is right and wrong. We can commend ourselves for trusting our feelings in these situations. For example, if we lose our job or if someone we love no longer loves us, we may feel insecure because work and love are essential components of happiness in the world as we know it. We do not yet know what lies ahead in the new world and so we feel a loss of security and comfort. But as fifth-dimensional beings, we know that abundance and love are universally available to us in every moment, and insecurity is not an issue. As most people are not yet into the fifth-dimensional vibration, feelings of fear around loss of work, income and love seem realistic. We need not berate ourselves. The greatest harm we inflict on our growth and psyches is to be negative about the beautiful beings that we are. Allow that many of our third-dimensional feelings are appropriate for the world we inhabit, and be accepting of who you are.

We are transitioning between two worlds, forced by circumstances in our lives to release the old ways of functioning and relating without yet being adept at the new. What a difficult time it seems to be. If you are caught between these feelings and realities, the best solution to counteract limiting emotions is to release your old belief systems and make decisions based on the feelings of your heart.

You can change your reliance on third-dimensional belief systems by being aware of their influence in your life and discarding them whenever they interfere with your feelings of Love. It takes great mindfulness to pay attention to what you are doing and how you are feeling at all times. You are already changing your belief systems or you would not be living so differently from your relatives. You trust your heart and your intuition more often than relying on societal programming. Using your intuition and your natural feelings means you are operating from a new set of rules, a new paradigm. Your mental self may tell you what you are saying and hearing is "weird," but your heart understands it as truth, and you choose to follow your heart. Following your heart moves you into a higher dimension.

In the fifth-dimensional reality where they exist, the dolphins don't use beliefs as a way of determining behavior. They are unconcerned about what people believe or think. One dolphin's insights are different than the others, so they do not compare ideas or thoughts and come up with a consensus of opinion to determine a common reality. It is only in the third dimension, where we rely on the intellect, that this is done. In the fifth, it is unimportant for one to "believe" in anything. Beings choose their reality in every moment and enjoy what they have created.

We find ourselves fluctuating between dimensions right now. Sometimes we experience time warps and memory lapses that cannot be rationally explained. Sometimes we have glimpses of another reality, a beautiful feeling, a sense of deep peace, an unexplained coincidence or occurrence. We realize we are being drawn inexplicably to different locations to gather with old souls we have not known in our third-dimensional reality. The groups of soul mates who know each other in fifth-dimensional worlds are coming together on the Earth plane to make the transformation together. Enjoy the gatherings and the surges of inspirational ideas and projects that result from these reunions.

Sometimes you feel sad because people you know are remaining in the limited third-dimensional way of understanding life. But realize that everything that is occurring to them is in perfect order too. They will awaken to their dormant possibilities OR they will remain in the three-dimensional world until they have learned their lessons there. Bless them and continue on your own path, confident in the knowledge that you have lost nothing, because achieving fifth-dimensional consciousness means you can access the third and fourth realities whenever you want to.

THE SPIRITUAL LIFE

In 1992 my friend Bonnie came from Colorado and we swam closely with dolphins every day. One afternoon as we sat overlooking the ocean in the lovely backyard of Dolphin House, we saw details in our surroundings that we could interpret as meaningful signs and symbols from nature. There were symbols in the clouds, the water patterns, the lava rocks, in the behavior of the birds, animals, and even the flying insects, the dragonfly and the wasp. Acknowledging and honoring the symbols rather than ignoring them, allowing them into our reality and staying immersed in a feeling-world rather than the cognitive rational one, we felt we were an integral part of everything in nature that was flourishing around us.

We felt a deep sense of caring, and an intuitive connection to nature and each other which made talking unnecessary. We understood each other completely. We had a mind connection that made words superfluous. We were filled with compassion and gratitude for our lives. Everything seemed in perfect, synchronistic order. We felt as joyful as children, laughing at the loving and amusing world that surrounded us. A sense of oneness prevailed.

The spiritual essence of this afternoon lingered and influenced our lives in the days following. Our minds expanded and our thoughts manifested immediately. Anything we needed was presented to us, our simplest desires actualized. Neighbors brought gifts of fruit and seafood unsolicited. We were not seeking many "things," since our hearts were at peace, but the slightest wish for some item would cause it to appear in our kitchen or in the yard. We experienced *spontaneous abundance*, an attribute of fourth and fifth-dimensional realities. No lack or need exists in those dimensions. We were filled with Mana, the life force. Our Mana interacted with everything around us, and through its intelligence provided for us. When you consciously integrate with the world around you, your wishes are granted. There is no separation because you and your world are one.

This is the world I want to experience every day. It requires honesty in everything I say and do, no deceptions, a stress-free life, harmony in friends and surroundings, good health and tuning-in to my own essence of love and my inner voice.

Ideally groups of people will be able to experience this reality together, living in communities and bringing the dolphins' teachings from the ocean onto the land, creating a space where we will swim, meditate, share, dance, tone, access our creativity, communicate with nature and open ourselves to the beauty that exists around us with all of its messages of joy and unity.

April 27, 1994

Today we left the pier at 8:00 a.m. and soon encountered more than three hundred Spinner dolphins who escorted our boat and remained with us for the entire morning. I was facilitating a Dolphin Connection Ocean Seminar Workshop for Yurika Nozaki, founder of Dolphin Love Communications, Tokyo, an organization which provides human/dolphin communication experiences for the people of Japan.

As the boat turned toward our home harbor at the end of the morning, one of my new friends, Tomoko, came to me and asked if the dolphins ever return things that people have lost in the water. I told her about the time I was kayaking in the ocean and, sliding out of the boat to have a swim, lost my paddle without realizing it. The dolphins did not bring it back to me, but they guided me over to the paddle, causing my head to bump against it. Only then did I realize it had floated away.

Another time I was with some friends and we all had kayaks. We left the kayaks tied together to a boat mooring while the dolphins swam with us. There were many small groups of dolphins that day, and we were each with our own friendly group. An hour passed, when we suddenly found ourselves at the same place with our different dolphin groups, and for the first time in that hour we looked up out of the water to see where we were. The dolphins had returned us to the mooring where our boats had been — but the kayaks were gone! We realized that they had come loose from the mooring and were drifting out to sea. Luckily the dolphins had noticed what was happening and had wisely brought us to the empty mooring so we could rescue our kayaks.

After hearing these stories, Tomoko told me that her jacket had slipped off the boat into the water about a half hour before. Rationally it seemed impossible that she could retrieve her jacket since we had been traveling at seven knots and were far from the place where she had first noticed her jacket missing. But knowing that many things are possible with the dolphins, I suggested she communicate with them through meditation right away and see what would happen.

As she closed her eyes and meditated on the deck, I wondered how I could help her. Because I have learned to ask for help, knowing that by asking you receive, I mentioned the lost jacket to the captain. He shut down the engines and dove off the boat to check the propellers. When he climbed back aboard, he had the jacket in his hand. Walking over to Tomoko, he softly tapped her on the shoulder, awakening her from her meditation. He held the jacket out to her. She opened her eyes and was incredulous that her request had been granted so quickly!

In the fifth dimension all wishes manifest into form as soon as a thought about them is conceived. It is instantaneous. Tomoko was experiencing fifth-dimensional Love within her own heart from the dolphin encounters and people around her. She made the request with sincerity to the dolphins, and her wish was honored.

To me it is a reminder that all of nature works together. When your heart is filled with love and trust as Tomoko's was, the forces of Light working on all levels assist each other in the fulfillment of your wishes…the dolphins, the ocean, the boat, the captain, Tomoko. Although there was a rational explanation for the return of her jacket, the incident stretched current beliefs about what is really possible when we sincerely ask for help. When we follow our higher consciousness, interactions between spiritual and physical matter happen regularly in response to our wishes.

DOLPHIN CONTACTS CHANGE OUR LIVES

Leading dolphin communication workshops, I notice that people go through specific, predictable changes as a result of prolonged contact with dolphins. The changes begin when the first dolphin contact has been made, whether it occurs in dreams, in meditation or elsewhere.

Then as people make contact with the dolphins in the ocean, a soul-searching begins. Participants look for meaning in their lives. They may realize that they are no longer interested in the work they are doing. Their jobs have become boring for them. They have worked long enough, they're at the age of retirement or they realize they never enjoyed their work at all. Suddenly they face the question: "Is this all there is in life?" Often they have acquired material belongings, raised children and noticed their parents' discontent at their unfulfilled lives. They realize they have neglected their own interests for the sake of others, and become strong enough to decide they no longer want to do this. They want to find personal meaning and happiness. In fact, it becomes a deep and driving need inside of them. An inner voice reminds them they have a purpose for their lives that they have not yet realized.

At this point, people often act on their decision to stop doing what they have been doing. They quit work or retire or sell their business or leave home, releasing the old belief systems that dictated their previous lifestyles. Realizing they are not their careers or their possessions or their children, they begin to understand who they really are. Sometimes this decision is prompted by an illness or divorce which makes them reevaluate their lives. Their higher selves call them to service to use their God-given talents, although they might not know what they are as yet. They feel the desire to change and to find more meaning in life. During this time people feel a mixture of freedom and loneliness. It is helpful for them to have supportive friends around.

Next, they consciously decide to enjoy life. People at this crossroad often sell something they own to have a little money to do whatever they've been missing. It takes a lot of trust to leave the old and choose to live a new life. Often, they travel for a while. They are searching. They don't yet know what fulfilling work/play they can do. Many of my friends decided to move near dolphins and become good swimmers and divers, giving up the stress in their lives and becoming healthy. Health is often very important during this stage of change. People realize they have mistreated their bodies while living apart from nature and in an environment that ignored their own natural rhythms of rest and play and work. They want to be free to spend each day however they choose.

Continuing to swim with the dolphins, people become aware of their own skills and talents and choose inspiring, fulfilling ways to express them. This new, unfolding work is based on their values of respect and love for themselves and their environment. It is usually altruistic, humanitarian, unique and creative. Many people become artists, photographers, alternative teachers, writers, dancers, musicians, poets, songwriters, dressmakers, singers, counselors, gardeners, storytellers or healers. They no longer choose to live in the city because their growing respect for Nature makes them want to live close to it. They choose to be with like-minded people and live in settings of beauty and harmony. They are interested in learning more about their dormant potentials and expressing their love for all of life. A sense of adventure permeates their lives as they begin to explore new activities and skills. They uncover parts of themselves they never knew existed. They learn about the real meaning of abundance and live with all of their deepest needs met. Their spiritual lives become the focus of their growth and work. The next time I meet these people, they are facilitating humanitarian projects in their communities. And they have completed the circle by teaching other people how to find fulfilling lives.

The dolphins are excellent examples of beings who live unencumbered by needs for materialistic acquisitions. Accessing other dimensional realities, they are happy and knowledgeable, living simply in community, having all they need to nurture themselves on multiple levels.

As a counseling psychologist, facilitating this type of awakening is very inspiring. It is a transformation achieved through the vibrational frequencies of joy and happiness. The interactions with the dolphins precipitate this experience by synchronizing the right and left hemispheres of our brains, opening us to our potentials as whole-brained beings. People are helped and supported through positive interactions such as play, laughter, movement, companionship and gentleness in settings of peace and beauty. The belief system that tells us suffering and pain are necessary ("No pain; no gain.") is obsolete. We learn to joyfully embrace change in our lives.

REWRITING OUR PASTS

In 1993, I visited Glastonbury, England to speak at the Geo Festival of Ascension Conference sponsored by the Glastonbury Circle. I was sharing the dolphins' teachings, including a startling phenomena that occurs frequently when people swim with wild dolphins — people experience their entire Earthly lives flashing through their minds as they swim.

In general, humans tend to focus on negative memories from their childhood such as feeling unloved, neglected and abused, and then live the rest of their lives as victims of those negative memories. But swimming with dolphins evokes *positive* childhood memories and encourages people to base their lives on those experiences instead. As people remember the times their families showed love and kindness to them, they understand that everyone has a role to fulfill in our individual and planetary evolution. Our parents and families are here to assist us in achieving wholeness. Often their roles are beyond our three-dimensional, limited ability to understand and it is important not to judge the rightness or wrongness of anyone's behavior. The person who has been elevated into higher consciousness by the dolphins then goes on to make the decision to live in love, to surrender regrets from the past and fears of the future, and to exist more fully in the present.

This is transformative for people — a small yet powerful shift. The dolphins have shown us that we can reframe our past and thereby change our present and our future. In our structured world of time and space, we understand our lives in a linear way in which we experience first our past, then our present and then our future. But looked at from the dolphins' point of view, we see that we actually transcend the time-space universe when we realize that our futures are already here. The Universe is not a linear system, it is holographic. All of our life experiences are occurring simultaneously and once we open to the expansive potentials of our minds, we will be able to access any of our life events at will. In dream states we do it already. However in three-dimensional reality it is too distracting for our evolving souls to access other realities, and so they are blocked from our awareness until we can learn to escalate our vibration. It is our "future" work that we incarnated on Earth to fulfill. For example, my future is already in place as a mediator between Earth beings and outer-planetary life forms, and my association with the dolphins supports that work. (More about this in Chapter 10.)

This dolphin thoughtform of rewriting one's past was to surface again when I met Elaine, an earthbound ET who owned the Bed and Breakfast where I was staying in Glastonbury. We resonated so compatibly with each other that our timely meeting projected us into an altered state of consciousness. I'm sure you've had this experience! We began relating to each other from cellular memories of a mutual "past" in the frequencies of the star system, Sirius. In that life Sirius-B was a formative field of creative energy for our present planet, Earth. Earth was created to support humanity's evolution into enlightenment, and meant to evolve and be uplifted with the rest of the solar system in the upcoming millennium. However things went into a downward spiral on Earth when we lost our spiritual focus. Elaine and I were shown that a decision was reached by the Celestial Hierarchy, or Solar Federation, to assist Earth in remembering its path by going backward in time and rewriting Earth's "history." Three energy ships of Light Beings were dispatched from Sirius to bring about the change and reseed the planet with a new "past." Peoples' consciousness was raised and they gained an awareness of the limitations which result from secular, materialistic lifestyles. Many of us are now radiating these new thought waves, the new Sound for the Earth, and the dolphins are here to help us.

5

DOLPHINS AND
WHALES AT PLAY

O ne of the dolphins' most intriguing behaviors is their
playfulness. The word "play" can be deceptive. We have an
understanding of play, and it is most often used when
referring to children. But from my contacts with the dolphins I feel
their play is a fantastic creative achievement involving holographic
imaging, bubble art, vibrational merging and geometric sounding. The
universe can be explained through mathematics, geometry and varying
vibratory oscillations. The dolphins model these universal energy
systems in their "playful" interactions with their environment.

My own introduction to dolphin-play began when the dolphins
realized that I could most easily receive their transmissions when I
was occupied physically and mentally by repetitive behaviors that
required my undivided attention. And so their ocean games with me
began.

October 4, 1990

A group of seven dolphins are swimming with JoAnn
and me. Moving along the surface, I see the sand below
with its multiple patterns and swirls and notice the occasional goat fish scavenging on the bottom. The shadowy
forms of the dolphins look like sea spirits through the
floating particles of white plankton in the water. They
have heard me singing and they come over to see us.

The water is murky this morning, visibility poor, and so I am straining my eyes to see the markings on the two nearest dolphins to identify who they are. They weave closer and closer to us, and I sense they are happy we are here. Their flukes are barely moving as they slow themselves to our pace. Looking for identifying scars on their bodies, I notice something on the fluke of the dolphin directly in front of me. It appears to be a large discoloration. What is it? I am concentrating and staring, kicking harder to get closer. Finally I can make out the shape and I see that the aberration on his tail is actually a leaf!

Slowly, the dolphin moves his fluke up and down at an angle, allowing me to easily view the large leaf draped over the edge. I realize that he is deliberately swimming in front of me to show me this leaf. At that moment he slows down and I reach out. It feels as though we're moving in slow motion. His fluke is now just inches from my outstretched hand. He half turns to look at me with one eye, sees that I am ready, and easily flicks the leaf directly in front of my face with great precision. A slight wave generated by his tail moves the leaf as I reach out for it and, miscalculating its position, I miss it. I reach again. It begins to float downward.

The dolphin meanwhile has turned in front of me and is watching. As I miss the leaf again, he circles me on the surface and I see that he is my good friend *Stitches* I then lunge down to retrieve the sinking leaf and finally catch it. He circles again. I try to throw the leaf back to him, but beneath the water you cannot really throw a leaf, and so it remains right in front of me. I move forward to try to wrap it around my swim fin in the way that *Stitches* had it around his fluke. He circles again very close, watching my every move. The leaf stays flattened against my fin. *Stitches* gives one last smile and slowly cruises into the blue.

I feel wonderful to have received this special gift, along with *Stitches'* exclusive attention. I keep the leaf, and when I return home I trace the shape of it in my research journal to have a permanent memory of *Stitches* and this wonderful day.

This was the beginning of many wonderful leaf game encounters between the dolphin and human pods. I often dive deeply with a leaf, releasing it below. The dolphins follow me down and one picks it up with his rostrum, flicks it to his dorsal fin and then his fluke. Swimming with it for a while on the surface, he soon releases it to me again. Sometimes he even spirals out of the water with the leaf flattened securely against his fin or his beak. On days after stormy nights we see nearly the entire pod swimming by with leaves decorating their pectoral and dorsal fins, as if they have the idea that these leaves are valuable to people. The dolphins also frequently play leaf tag among themselves and teach the game to their babies. Playing the leaf game for hours, I learned it is their way to keep me relaxed, with an open mind and feeling happy, so they can easily send information directly to my cells as we play together.

September 17, 1997

Twenty-one dolphins arrive. They are jubilant and reflecting my joyful feelings. We play the leaf game together. As usual they tease me, by catching the leaf just moments before my outstretched hand can close on it. *Three Spot* takes the leaf deep, releasing it. As I dive to retrieve it, he circles and reaches it first. I ease off my dive strokes, thinking he has it, only to see him purposely miss it and wait for me to continue on down. By now I am short on air, but he is waiting, so I kick my way deeper down — only to have him again swim toward the leaf and easily lift it out of my reach. Kicking quickly to the surface to breathe, I look down at him beneath me. He doesn't seem to have the leaf. Where is it? I look around. Did another dolphin pick it up? No one around. Could it have floated to the surface? No, not there. Where is it? *Three Spot* slowly drifts up beside me and does an easy roll, making me laugh. There's the leaf! He is hiding it! He has it underneath him, plastered flat on his belly, held there by the pressure of the water as he swims forward. By now I'm really laughing, causing water to flood my mask and make me laugh even more. He knows he fooled me and we both appreciate the joke.

One dolphin named *Beauty Mark* is very possessive of her leaves that she finds floating on the surface or lying on the sand below. She treats the leaves like a treasure.

April 12, 1994

Beauty Mark swims over, proudly displaying a leaf. Her identifying mark is a black dot visible beneath her left eye. She is playing alone with her leaf in her customary way, releasing it and catching it again. Playing right in front of me and below me. I make some attempts to catch the free-floating leaf, swimming as fast as I can and diving. But she easily turns around and glides by, collecting it as she passes. The dolphins nearby are following her in a playful mood. A juvenile named *Wrinkley* quickly sweeps down and catches her leaf on his fin and swims away. The chase begins! It is obvious that *Beauty* wants her leaf back. She is relentless. She won't let him alone, chasing him and bumping softly into him. Together they zoom ahead of me and the rest of the pod, and then they turn and zoom back remaining in sight. Finally *Wrinkley* loses the leaf and Beauty catches it on her pectoral fin with great finality. Now she swims back to me, playing her tantalizing game again as I leave *Stitches* and the rest of the pod to follow her. This time releasing the leaf and slowly circling to retrieve it, she underestimates how close the leaf is to me. While her back is turned, I silently pick up speed and snatch it away from her approaching rostrum with only inches to spare! Then I swim on the surface with the leaf, waving it in my hand. Sometimes I hold it above my head, out of the water. She never gives up, but stays next to me. Looking into her eye, I suddenly feel badly knowing how much the leaf means to her. So I immediately dive and release it below, watching as she quickly retrieves it. She seems so happy to have it back on her pectoral fin. Silently I communicate to her, "I would never keep your leaf. I won't tease you and swim away with it. Everything I have I will share with you. I love you."

She stays close to me swimming quietly at my side. I feel so much love for her. Then she slowly moves ahead and swims in front of me. As I watch, she wiggles her pectoral fin, rubbing it back and forth against her side until a fragment tears off and floats back to me. I reach out and catch it easily — a small piece of leaf from her leaf, now we each have one. "Thank you dear *Beauty*. I know you love me too."

In addition to leaves, the dolphins will play with anything they find in the ocean including plastic, fish and seaweed. One day the dolphins were playing with a large jellyfish, swimming directly at its pulsating jelly belly and breaking it into pieces. When they noticed me swimming over, *Whitey* caught it on her rostrum and proudly brought it to me. Not wanting to be stung, I quickly removed my swim fin and used it to push the jellyfish back! The dolphins apparently were not hurt by the stinging tentacles. On another day, my friend Cindy realized the dolphins wanted to play the catch-and-give-back game with her. Since there was no leaf nearby, she removed the top of her bathing suit and let them play with that. They enjoyed the colorful cloth so much she began to wonder if she would get it back. Since it was her new bathing suit, when they finally brought it back, she kept it. Bathing suits are pricey these days!

Footage of "the leaf game" can be seen on the Dolphin Connection video, *Open To The Sea*, available from our office.

FALSE KILLER WHALE'S GIFT

A friend of mine who is a wonderful well-known photographer, researcher and cetacean friend, tells an amazing story about some false killer whales he encountered in the water in Hawaii. He saw a group of them on the horizon being very active and even leaping out of the water. He approached them in his boat and then entered the water to observe their interactions. Immediately some of the whales focused their attention on him and began to swim fast toward him (at least it seemed very fast to him!) They had apparently just caught and were eating a 250-300 pound tuna when he arrived. One of the whales approached him with a large piece of the fish still in its mouth. The whale swam right at him at great speed and then (happily) stopped just a few feet in front of him. As my friend watched with a mixture of concern, curiosity and awe, the whale released the piece of fish in front of him. It was such an obvious gift — the whale was sharing his meal. My friend took the fish and held it in his hand for a while. The pseudorca did not leave, so he had the feeling he was supposed to give the fish back. As best he could, he pushed the big chunk of fish in front of him. The whale quickly took it up and swam away with it. Similar to our leaf game, this whale-initiated interaction used the fish as a way to exchange a gift and to communicate with another species…us.

BUBBLE ART

The dolphins often play with bubbles of air that they make from their blowholes. We have seen them make twelve-inch bubbles which they gently push around beneath the surface. They treat these delicate orbs with great care and are able to keep them in bubble form for as long as two minutes before they intentionally burst them by biting them or pushing them to the surface. Sometimes a dolphin releases a large bubble from his blowhole and then gently blows a series of small bubbles into the larger one. It is very beautiful to watch. On many occasions they seem to do this just to entertain us, as if they know we enjoy their art.

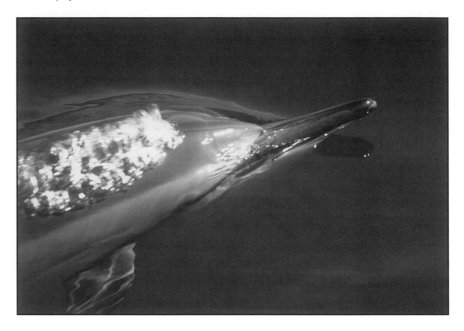

I've also seen them make a bubble wall, where a group of dolphins releases a barrage of small bubbles in such profusion that they fill a fifteen-foot area and make visibility through it impossible. Sometimes my friends and I mimic this behavior by diving together in a line, curving upward and blowing as many bubbles as possible out of our snorkels. Although we have not yet been able to duplicate their amazing walls, we create a beautiful vision with many bubbles ascending around us.

The dolphins have a wonderful ability to control the size, shapes and quantity of the bubbles they make as they eliminate air from their blowholes underwater. Once, a group of ten dolphins swimming beneath me simultaneously released a group of large, eight-inch bubbles which began wobbling slowly up toward the surface. I stopped swimming to observe the silvery, undulating discs magically rising. When the bubbles were within five feet of me I watched in amazement as a line of small, fast bubbles came skyrocketing up from the dolphins below, and hit the large bubbles — every one — causing them to burst in the water like bottles in a shooting gallery! What a beautiful sight, as the large, silvery baubles burst into sparkling, popping rainbows and the small bubbles scattered in all directions. How had they done that? Such coordination, combined with a great sense of play. I felt they had created that vision just for my observation and amusement. I was duly impressed.

SINGER DOLPHIN

The dolphin named *Singer* teaches me dolphin sounds. As is common for these dolphins, she teaches while we play and she has developed a unique game with me. She begins the game by swimming approximately five feet below the surface and making high-pitched whistles. With each sound she emits, she releases a stream of tiny bubbles from her blowhole. Then, as I mimic her sounds, she slowly moves further ahead of me while we continue to whistle in tandem. Eventually she is swimming beyond my ability to see her, but I can still hear her.

I follow along, led only by her trail of small bubbles. Here's the extra challenge she creates for me: I am to continue to swim fast, following her and imitating her sounds which she makes more and more frequently. She picks up speed and leaves me a bubble trail which slowly rises to the surface, breaking and disappearing. Since she is only a few feet below the surface, the bubbles have a short lifespan before they burst. I need to swim fast, or I will lose her trail!

She turns and dives and makes circles, always staying just far enough ahead to allow me to follow the last series of bubbles that reveal her direction. We do this for over an hour, and it is quite a workout because I need to swim fast, breathe and mimic her high-pitched sounds at the same time as I swim on the surface with my head underwater. It is a game designed to enhance my breathing and endurance in the ocean. It makes me laugh because her swim path is so erratic, as she weaves, dives and somersaults along! *Singer* has a great sense of humor.

May 16, 1995

Today the dolphins arrived at 6:35 a.m. There were eighteen in the first group that swam to meet me. Four juveniles were very playful and funny, diving and nearly crashing into each other (and me). Then another group of thirty-five swam by. It was Pod C with *Pacmom* and her baby (not so small any more), and *Moonsmile, Pseudo-Zac* and *Ragged Fin.*

Seaweed Mouth released a single, large bubble, about an eight-inch radius. He floated up vertically with it, keeping the bubble at eye level. Suddenly he whacked it with his mouth and it immediately divided into four perfect bubbles…no extra foam or little bubbles, just four perfect small bubbles. Amazing to see.

What was the message? *"Changing form."* One unit of matter had been converted into four units of the same quality, element and total volume — a visual image to awaken my dormant knowledge of transforming energy and shape-shifting.

SASKIA'S STORY

I have seen some amazing bubble art created by the dolphins, some of which would have been difficult to believe had I not seen it myself. I often wonder how they can coordinate and control their breathing so precisely.

One day my friend Saskia, a dolphin researcher and child psychologist from Holland, returned from a day spent out in the ocean on a Zodiac, and shared this story.

"We drove the Zodiac not very far from shore when we saw Spotted dolphins. At first I thought there were only a few, then it became clear that it was a big group — maybe a hundred, spread out over a large area.

"I went in and out of the water many times. Although most of the dolphins were 'minding their own business' there were a few dolphins engaging with me in dances very similar to my experiences with the Spinners in the bay. Two babies zoomed up to me several times. All morning I had noticed that they were making bubbles that were coming up in front of the boat. I thought to myself: So, it's not only the Spinners who play the bubble game.

"I was very surprised though when I swam back to the boat and saw a huge 'screen' of bubbles coming up towards me. The visibility was great that day, but all I saw below me was deep blue. No trace of dolphins. The bubblescreen, about as big as a bedsheet, consisted of tiny bubbles and came from the deep, up towards me. When it came closer, I saw it became the shape of a dolphin — about three times life-size. It became even more amazing when the back of the 'dolphin' was about to touch the surface. It arched like a dolphin does, to let the blowhole surface first. Then the bubbles dissolved into the air.

"I had to hold on to the Zodiac to catch my breath, having a hard time believing that what I had just seen had really happened!"

Thinking about this experience of Saskia's, and my own experiences of dolphins and bubbles, I am reminded of the illusional quality of our present lives. There are amazing events occurring all around us, just beyond our ability to believe. The dolphins are gently helping us to open our minds.

DIVING THROUGH BUBBLE HOOPS

One sunny fall day, five dolphins from Pod B were swimming gaily with me. *Notches* made a beautiful stream of multi-sized bubbles as he swam next to me. He then dove down in a straight line, cutting sharply through the water, releasing many bubbles, and making a constant stream of rising bubbles around himself. Immediately I followed him, diving into the ascending profusion of glistening bubbles. They tickled my body. I felt like part of a dream vision.

As the five dolphins continued to accompany me, they dove and swam near the sand on the bottom. I was floating above them, watching. My attention was caught by a thin emission of bubbles that suddenly appeared below me. As I focused my eyes on it, I saw the dolphins had somehow made a circle of tiny bubbles that was floating slowly up towards me like a big basketball hoop. The dolphins were weaving among themselves beneath it, when they turned to look at me. Suddenly I had the impulse to dive. I jackknifed down and slowly, gracefully dove through their thirty-inch hoop ring, being careful not to break it with my fins as I exited and turned around. The bubble continued rising and then broke apart at the surface. The dolphins meanwhile circled around me and began chattering in the way they do when they are excited about something I have done. I had the distinct impression they were saying, "Look! The human has intelligence. She knows how to swim through the hoop!"

Recently I saw footage of a Humpback whale making bubble rings. His rings are five to ten feet across, and can be seen through the blue water as huge white halos ascending. Reaching the surface they explode with powerful bursts of air and spray. The whale making these bubbles even swims through the center of the ring, appearing very playful.

My friends and I practice making bubble rings, expelling air through our mouths underwater, allowing the bubble hoops to expand like shimmering rings of mercury, and diving through them as they slowly rise to the surface. Suchi is the most proficient. She can make ten rings in one dive with only one breath! Recently she began blowing two rings in succession, which often make an infinity symbol as they ascend and merge. Here is a photograph Suchi took of our friend Lorn making a bubble ring.

September 26, 1990

I notice the dolphins swimming in a westerly direction away from me as I enter the water today, so I begin singing my signature song. They come over and cruise below my friend, Stan and me. Very noisy...high whistles and sonar, checking us out, then they disappear. Stan is new to them. What will they do next? They visit two other snorkelers. I often observe this type of behavior. Whenever new swimmers come into the bay, the dolphins swim over as if to greet them. They do the same with tourist boats and kayaks. Soon they return to us, moving as a unit, a dreamlike vision in the blue. The entire pod of thirty-five are here. We swim as One. There are some tiny babies. One in particular looks like it was just born. It's only eighteen inches long, with no identifying marks. Another older baby is very active, swimming wildly around me. She has long wavy scratch marks on her right flank. I name her *Wavy*. She jumps out of the water right in front of me and seems so pleased to show off for me.

Many dolphins are touching and making love as usual. I am thinking about how frequently I see mating between dolphins, and as I think this three pairs of dolphins begin to mate directly in front of me. It is quite unusual because they are all at the surface, all in full view and all mating at the same time. They glide together, pairing with each other not two feet from my mask. They are belly to belly, making love, and as one pair passes before my eyes they separate slightly. I can easily see the male's penis placed in the female's vagina. I am amazed at their lesson in anatomy, seemingly in response to the thoughts on my mind! It is common for the dolphins to respond to my thoughtforms like this.

I am with a group of five dolphins on the surface, but I sense there are others deep below. I have always enjoyed the dolphins' ability to make large, small, and profuse air bubbles from their blowholes; and as I think this, I notice a stream of small bubbles flowing upward from the blue depths. Is it coming from a dolphin? I can't see a thing down there, it's too murky today. Usually I make a point of investigating any unknown objects or movements on the bottom by diving down. But I am enjoying the group of dolphins swimming next to me, so I decide to stay with them uninterrupted. Another glistening stream of small bubbles rises from the blue below to tempt me, but I continue to swim ahead.

Now I see a group of six or eight dolphins thirty feet below and a little ahead of me. Suddenly I notice two perfect six-inch bubbles rising from them. The bubbles are twelve inches apart, parallel to each other and moving straight up in the water, wobbling like mercury the way that underwater bubbles do. I don't know if one or two dolphins released them, but I watch them floating slowly upward, side by side about fifteen feet ahead of me. Like a child I have the desire to catch these bubbles of air. So I continue to swim vigorously forward with hands out-stretched, palms down. At first I think the two bubbles will surface before I reach them, but then to my delight I see they are perfectly timed with my speed in the water. My hands and the bubbles meet at the same time on the water's surface. They arrive, one in each of my hands. I am completely focused on this simple but concentrated exercise, when suddenly I become aware of these thoughts: *"We the dolphins are down here, parallel to you as we both move through the deep consciousness of galactic evolution. If you will continue to move forward without distraction or dalliance, with your hands and hearts open to receive, our wisdom will be understood by you. Every-thing moves with perfect and correct timing in the Univer-sal plan, everything comes together at the precise moment of divine convergence. We are here to assist you and to serve your best interests which are also the best interests of the planet. So proceed with Love, Trust, and Faith that everything you need to know will come into your hands at precisely the correct moment in Universal time. The time is at hand."*

I receive the bubbles and close my fingers around them. They burst and their air of wisdom is released into the ocean.

The dolphins continue to spin and turn all around us. We dive and spiral together. They trust me in their midst. We look into each other's eyes...theirs so deep and dark, mine a face mask with blue eyes inside. They swim in front of me, allowing me just enough room to continue moving forward. We narrowly miss each other, yet we never collide. I allow them to choose the distance between us. I have stopped slowing my pace on their behalf. I swim confidently into their midst and yet we rarely touch. They have it measured to a hair's breadth, passing in front of me with mere inches to spare! I am so relaxed with them, trusting their guidance. I feel the thoughts... *"Release limiting beliefs about control and safety. Allow the higher reality with its expanded consciousness and wisdom to lead you into freedom and intimate contact with each other and with us."*

A dolphin swims by with a torn leaf on his pectoral fin. I think he wants to play so I pick up speed and reach out for the leaf. I nearly touch his side as I reach, but he turns ever so subtly to one side and moves slowly but surely away. I feel some disappointment that I came so close to the leaf and did not get it. Suddenly the same dolphin is right next to me. I see a leaf on his fluke. Is it the same leaf? No. There's the torn leaf still on his pectoral fin. Where did he get another one? He gazes at me deeply. Is that a twinkle in his eye? I feel the words... *"There's no need to grab for gifts. There are plenty of them, more than you know of. They will all be yours eventually. There are many more where these came from. Let's play together freely in perfect harmony in the ocean of other dimensions."*

November 17, 1991

The dolphins arrive at 6:44 a.m. today. After having a hot drink, I swim a half mile to the area we refer to as "the three pyramids" outlined in boulders on the cliff. The sun is just rising over the hill and it is a welcome sight after three days of rain.

The dolphins were at the three pyramids, but by the time I arrive they have circled back toward shore. I tread water and wait, knowing this is Pod C behavior. They usually sonar, have a discussion about me and then swim over! Sure enough, they swim back, playing and diving as they come. No hurry. After about fifteen minutes there are eleven dolphins beneath me. I hear soft whistles being exchanged. I wonder if these are the only ones here today as I scan their bodies for identifying marks. They cruise on by.

All at once three dolphins surface at my side nearly colliding with me. I am momentarily surprised and then filled with great joy as I recognize my old friend, *Exx* from Pod A. He is swimming apart from Pod C with *Fancy* and *Ribbon. Fancy* and *Exx* sandwich me between them and *Ribbon* swims to the right of *Exx.* I have to lower my body in the water as we swim, because they are trying to swim over me! They are getting as close as they possibly can. They touch me over and over again with the sides of their heads. They stay with me on the surface, occasionally diving slowly. If I don't dive with them, they immediately return to my side. When I do follow them in a dive, they watch me with interest while staying in front and leading me down, turning their heads slightly so their eyes remain in contact with mine. They do not spin and circle me the way *Bentley* and *Two Wave* do. These three dive sedately together, swimming deeper than I can go.

I return to the surface and they remain cruising along the bottom for a few minutes before floating slowly up, positioning themselves alongside me again. As usual, the dolphins seem to love having me in their midst as long as I am gentle, graceful and swimming synchronistically with them. Always aware of this, I match their pace and mood. We swim rhythmically together for two hours, enjoying the benefit of the natural water flowfield we are creating. Occasionally other people come along, but the dolphins guide me away, and we continue our interaction uninterrupted.

Ten dolphins are now below us. I notice a large area of churning water in their midst. Looking more closely, I see a great circle of tightly packed bubbles rising amid a sea of tiny free-floating bubbles, covering an area five feet around. A large eighteen-inch bubble grows out of the profusion of tiny bubbles As the cluster rises, the large bubble expands and suddenly bursts, leaving a clear passageway of undisturbed water from the sand below to the surface, surrounded by a frenzy of tiny bubbles. I react immediately, diving precisely into this amazing underwater "tunnel," surrounded by a foamy bubble-storm. Remaining in place upside down, all I can see is glittering lights sparkling in the underwater sunlight. Dreamily, the six-foot column of bubbles ascends around me. Slowly I swim to the bottom of it and then turn to go up for air while the bubbles continue to drift and pop at the surface. It reminds me of a transportation beam from Star Trek. Beam me up dolphins!

6

THE POWER OF SOUND

Occasionally when people come to my home to swim among dolphins they have an expectation that they will hold on to a dolphin's dorsal fin and be taken for a ride. I explain that these free-swimming dolphins do not do this, in fact they resist anyone aggressively trying to grab hold of them. I had the same fantasy when I first met them. I looked at their silky, smooth skin and longed to touch them and even to hug them. After all, *Flipper* allowed people to do that! Well I quickly learned that the Spinner dolphins were not interested in encouraging this type of interaction. Instead they communicated to me:

"We are here to teach you to move beyond the limits of the five senses, and we encourage you to communicate with us in the unexplored domains of the sixth sense and beyond...to merge in vibrational worlds of communication with us and all beings. Now your senses are being heightened and expanded. For example, you will begin to smell images, hear feelings and see sounds! Your entire body is becoming a sensory organ and all of its senses will interact with each other."

GOING BEYOND THE FIVE SENSES

One of the ways the dolphins communicate is with their sonar. The word sonar is an acronym for SOund, NAvigation and Ranging. The dolphins transmit high-frequency sound waves through water and register the vibrations that reflect back to them from objects in their path. Besides using sonar to receive and send messages, I have seen dolphins use their sonar with precision to stun small fish, causing the fish to fall to the bottom of the bay. The dolphin circles down and gently nudges the inert fish, until the fish regains consciousness and begins to move. Sometimes, when the fish tries to groggily swim away, the dolphin zaps it again with his sonar and the fish falls back to the bottom. I have never seen a dolphin eat the fish during this demonstration, only play with it and reveal to me the effectiveness of his sonar.

Many people have experienced the energy of dolphin sonar scanning their bodies. Usually you can feel it most easily on the back of your neck. This is a tool the dolphins use to balance energies and assist in healing. There are uses for sonar in vibrational communication and dispersion and assimilation of energy fields that we have yet to understand. The dolphin frequencies energize my body, accelerating my physical strength and endurance in the water. Along with expanding my capacity to perceive and understand more, dormant capabilities beyond my five senses are awakened, enabling fascinating communications with other species.

As you grow familiar with the vibrational frequency of cetaceans, you become able to find them in the ocean. I often swim with my eyes closed and use my "sonar" to locate the dolphin pods. I focus on my third eye and visualize a beam of light streaming from my forehead. When I am on boats in Hawaii or in foreign waters, I stand on the bow, close my eyes and use my sonar to scan the depths of the water around me to locate dolphin or whale pods. I then send out a beam of radiant White Light directly to them with the hope that they will choose to investigate this beam and follow it back to the boat. An important element of this sonaring process is to send feelings of Love at the same time. To keep myself in a focused field of Love, I think about and feel my love for the dolphins or whales while sending dual beams of energy to them, one from my heart and one from my third eye. The dolphins and whales, sensitive to multiple frequencies, follow the Light beam to our boat to play with us. The choice is always up to them. When the dolphins and whales arrive, the joy of the people mingles with the leaping, porpoising activity of the dolphins, creating a tremendous human-cetacean celebration.

THE SECRETS OF SOUND — SOUNDS THAT STOP TIME

I believe that the dolphins were trying to make contact with me in the 1970s when I lived in California, but I was unaware of them. The awareness developed slowly and subtly with my exposure to the cetacean-infused thoughtforms of Dr. John Lilly, world renowned dolphin researcher and scientist. I did not know him personally at the time, but our paths had crossed energetically as we made contact with entities from Sirius called "The Nine" at Esalen Institute, California.

My initiation to the power of sound occurred on a clear, sunny Saturday, in the spring of 1978 at *Oceansong* bookstore in California. This shop is a lovely place with many interesting books and beautifully crafted items from different cultures. I had gone there to browse among the books with my friend, Tysen. We were standing side by side looking at books we had chosen, when I felt an unusual sensation pass through my body. I quickly looked up and around to determine what it was. Seeing nothing unusual, I returned to my book, but I had become aware that music was playing in the background on the store's stereo system. The beautiful, clear tones of a flute, moving up the scale, surrounded me. Then a single high-pitched note commanded my full attention. I became entranced by its pure sweetness and clarity. As the flute played this note, it resonated through the store and I felt it move through my body like a soft electric current, momentarily creating a tingling cloud of energy around me, immersing me in it.

Trying to ignore the feeling, I returned to my book, but soon became aware of the same series of beautiful flute sounds being played again. This time I gave them my full attention, and as the notes accelerated, moving up the scale toward that same sound, I felt my personal energy field moving into resonance with the high-pitched note. Being unfamiliar with this vibrational field, I chose to separate my energy-system from the momentum of the musical tone, willing myself to remain unaffected by it.

At that moment, the same clear, high tone resonated from the speakers. It suddenly felt as if time had expanded. The note seemed to be held for a long time. Then to my astonishment, as I looked around I realized that no one in the store was moving! Everyone was frozen in place, motionless, suspended in whatever position they had been in before the tone began, their bodies and expressions inanimate.

This was unsettling. I tend to not like things I can't understand (especially back then!) Tysen was standing next to me looking down at his book, one hand in the process of turning a page. He was not moving. I turned around and saw the store manager at the cash register, smiling at a customer, one hand in the cash drawer while the immobile customer waited for her change. All around the store people were in different poses and stances, all stopped in action. It felt eerie, as though I was surrounded by mannequins.

Suddenly, the tone ended and everyone began moving again, seemingly unaware that anything unusual had occurred. I was flabbergasted! I turned to Tysen and demanded an explanation. Why had he just stood there without moving, why hadn't he acted normal? He looked at me strangely and asked what I was talking about. I was frustrated and tried to explain what I had witnessed, but he couldn't understand, and I realized I sounded a bit crazy. Trying to find comfort in a familiar behavior, I resumed perusing the book in my hand, but my mind was trying to comprehend what I had just experienced.

Then, to my distress and concern, a few minutes later another bizarre experience occurred. Tysen was reading a book by John Lilly. I had never heard of Dr. Lilly at that time and had no interest in his books or in dolphin research. I didn't even know how to swim, and was actually afraid of deep water. Tysen evidently was enjoying Lilly's book, which compared the human brain to a computer, and he passed me the book so that I could look at it. But I was still preoccupied by what had just occurred, and after a quick glance I laid the book on the shelf in front of me, not sure if Tysen wanted it back or not. A couple of minutes passed, as we continued to stand side by side looking through different books. Then Tysen asked me for the Lilly book, since he had decided to buy it. It's right here, I thought, and reached for it on the shelf — only to find it was not there. I had just put it down, we had not moved, no one had come over, but the book was gone.

I looked on the floor, I looked behind the shelf, I looked among all the other books. It had disappeared! Could someone have come over without my knowing it? I asked the people around me over and over if they had seen the book. I repeated John Lilly's name so many times he now felt like an old friend. But the other customers only looked at me strangely (second time that day!) Finally I found the store manager, and asked *him* for the book. He went to where Tysen was still standing and began looking for the book. He knew he had a copy of it. He searched all over, he checked his computer listings and finally he looked at me suspiciously. It could not be found.

We left the store without it. The book had disappeared, in a split second, maybe even in a frozen or accelerated moment of time, with no rational explanation. The "disappearing book" incident served to expand my belief system to a realization that there was a lot more going on around me than I knew. These occurrences happen to all of us, but we forget them because they are outside our belief systems. It's as if we have coded the "mind-in-our-cells" with triggers that awaken us when we experience certain high frequencies around us. Our higher selves, like guidance systems, lead us to these triggering events according to our inner clocks. Eventually our increasing awareness causes us to understand what is happening, and to recall the significance of it. In 1978 I was not aware of my future work with the dolphins' high-pitched frequencies, nor their acoustic imagery, but my cosmic guidance was initiating a wake-up call within me.

Eventually I learned there is a type of energy wave called a *telepathic wave* that is similar to a radio wave and can transmit sound and images. High-frequency sound waves can enhance this process and certain low-frequency waves can interfere. During my experience at the bookstore, a telepathic wave was transmitted, so powerful it was able to override the frequencies of all the human forms and minds in the vicinity. The high-frequency sound of the flute was used to assist the process. Information was then communicated to me on physical and nonphysical levels through this telepathic wave. The sound served as a vibrational wake-up call to align me with a memory pattern related to my purposes on Earth.

The next Monday at my apartment in Orange County, I received a flyer in the mail from the Featherpipe Ranch in Montana, inviting me to a workshop — with John Lilly. I enrolled immediately although

I had no interest in the subject matter: Dolphins. At the Ranch, many people shared stories of the unusual events that had led to their attending the gathering. One person mysteriously found one of John's books laying on her bed at home, with no clues to its origin. Another person was there because John's book had fallen off a shelf in a bookstore and hit him on the head. I was in good company! During that lovely time in the green hills of Montana, John and Toni Lilly played tapes of dolphin sounds every day and soon the dolphins were in my dreams nightly. But it would take six more years for me to truly wake up to the call of the dolphins and meet them in person.

THE SOUNDS OF THE DOLPHINS

Alfred Tomatis, author of *The Conscious Ear*, says that we cannot make a sound or vibration until we can first hear it or feel it. Humans can hear in the range of 20-20,000 cycles per second (cps Hertz). Dolphins can hear up to 200,000 cps. So they hear and feel a much wider vibrational field than we humans are presently capable of experiencing, including vibrational fields remaining in air and water from aeons ago. They are in contact with the ancient information stored in the oceans and in the cosmos. With each day that we swim with them, we begin to know and become familiar with these other worlds that they so easily and naturally travel through.

As you swim you tone up your body. All the cells in your body are toned. Not only is it toned by the dolphins and whales, it is toned by swimming in the water itself. The water is composed of molecules that are filled with vibrational information that enters your own information system through the water molecules in your own body. Water passes through and around the planet and its life forms and contains the knowledge of the planet. In addition, radiations are transmitted into the ocean from other cosmic forces, planets, stars, comets, sun flares, energy bands, eclipses and extra intelligent life transmissions. Water is never destroyed. It is only recycled. It remains here as an ancient source of wisdom, a molecular library. The dolphins and whales access this Akashic Record of Earth.

The dolphins have encouraged me to learn more about the Secrets of Sound. Swimming among them for hours I try to mimic their vocalizations. It is a natural yearning while living among them, to speak as they do and to speak with them. I know that my ability to make sounds is closely associated with my ability to hear sounds, and it is easy for me to improve my hearing because of my good friend, *Lumpy*. *Lumpy* is a dolphin who has a few notches out of his lower backbone, creating a deformed, lumpy appearance on his spine. Soon after meeting him it became evident that he was conducting research on me! Swimming alongside me, he makes high-pitched whistles and I attempt to copy them. This we do easily, for a while, until he begins to move just a little faster and stay just a bit ahead of me. I continue to mimic him, he continues to move further away, until finally I can no longer see him. But still able to hear and follow his sounds, I continue to be his echo until he is too far away for me to hear. My silence alerts *Lumpy* that I have reached the extent of my hearing capabilities.

After a short silence, *Lumpy* is suddenly right next to me again, starting all over, making sounds and encouraging me to practice as he moves further and further away. This time he makes the sounds closer and closer together until I barely have time to finish making my sound before I have to concentrate intently on hearing his next one. To keep up with him, I also have to breathe fast, inhaling rapidly before exhaling the air with my whistle sound. Doing this through a snorkel as I swim as silently as possible so I can listen carefully, breathe and tone takes great concentration and energy. *Lumpy* is helping me to listen better, to discern many more variations of sounds, and to refine my inner and outer hearing skills.

ACOUSTIC IMAGERY

In addition to receiving dolphins' high-pitched sounds, I have identified another type of dolphin communication, which I call Acoustic Imagery. The waveform patterns of specific dolphin sounds have vibrational frequencies which communicate information through pictures. The pictures show a visual/sensual representation of the dolphin message. The images encode our cells through pictorial sound waves. The sound pictures imprint images holographically onto our cells and the intelligence within the cells then translates the acoustic image into our minds through the language of feelings and sensations. When we speak in pure tones, our words create pictures of our verbalizations. The pictures of our voice patterns can now be depicted on computer monitors, as this new technology is explored by healing-with-sound professionals.

Looking at dolphins' behavior leads to many questions. Why are they so fascinated by vibrational worlds? Do they live for pleasure and beauty? Is there a beneficial reason to create these holographics? Do the vibrational forms have an essence of their own that also interacts with the environment just as our own essence does? What are the dolphins conveying to the environment with their forms? Or are they content just to involve themselves in mystical play with shapes and colors, like computer artists creating sound and light technologies?

There is more occurring here than we realize. As part of the transformation our Earth will be replicated holographically (with *Holy Graphics!*) and we will find ourselves living in an acoustic image, a new twin world, one without pollution, war and greed. We will easily shift into this refined holographic field that contains all the spiritual attributes of life on Earth. The dolphins are preparing us by playfully shifting realities in the ocean and communicating with us holographically.

June 20, 1991

The dolphins are teaching me to imitate their high-pitched sounds and whistles. They sing out their tones and I repeat them back as best I can. In the process, I listen more and more intently to them. I am astounded at the variation of sounds I hear, so much more than mere "noise" in the water. Their sound creates a feeling that moves through my entire body. It creates a subtle change in the environment around me that is amplified by the ocean. I believe the dolphins use vibrational emissions to change the vibratory field around them. Trying to dupli-cate their sound means trying to create that same power-ful field in the water. It must move out from me and touch them in the same way their sounds move out from them and affect me. Vibrational healing feels like this.

As I respond, the resulting communication is one of a mutually changed environment. It seems to be a game the dolphins enjoy, varying it from time to time and playing with the sensation of creating new spaces. Can you imag-ine the fun you can have when you play with your environment, changing it as quickly as a thought?

Today I begin by mimicking them and by listening. My close proximity to them, my immersion in their world, helps me to feel like one of their pod. Just being in the ocean makes me more alert and aware. Everything becomes crystal clear. It is such a change from my life on the land. I hear the water sounds, the fish eating the coral, the waves on the rocks, the boats creaking and bumping at their moorings, the spoutings from the blowholes of the pod, the splashing of other swimmers. I feel the shadow of clouds crossing in front of the sun, the wind and the water currents, the tide, the bubbles rushing along the edges of my moving body. I hear the seabirds, the voices of distant people carrying clearly over the water's surface, the sounds of motors, the rush of water against my ears as I glide along, the squeaking of my face mask as I dive. Messages from the living earth that we receive during our daily lives may be repressed by our schooling and enculturation, but contact with another environment, the ocean, brings me a newness and alertness that is conducive to expanded awareness. It is in this aquatic environment that we will understand communication systems to assist people in accessing many realms. Learning it in the ocean and then bringing it to land.

SINGING IN THE OCEAN

The dolphins make many sounds in the water. Our ears can only hear a subset of these sounds because the dolphins are capable of vocalizing in frequencies beyond our present physical ability to hear. However the rest of our body can "hear" them all, and I have experienced their sounds as healing whether I can hear them with my ears or not. Dolphin sounds, like deep meditation, positively affect body, mind and emotions. The high-pitched whistles of the Spinner dolphins and the deep tones of the Humpback whales vibrate messages through the bones and the cells of my body. They send their tones into the water, an ideal conduit for sound waves, affecting my metabolism and energy levels beneficially. On most days I can sense these sounds on the skin of my body.

I am often asked by media personnel: Why do people want to swim with dolphins? And how are people healed in the water with dolphins? I believe part of the explanation is due to this special balancing/healing frequency the dolphins naturally transmit to us in the ocean.

It has been shown that the organs of our body each vibrate a different note on the scale. Together all of the organs and bones and elements of our body create one harmonic tone that is our individual note, or "signature sound." Research presently being conducted indicates that when we are psychologically or physiologically out of balance, there is disharmony in our organs which can be detected and remedied through exposure to a balancing tone. In other words, the correct tone can alleviate illness and emotional distress and allow the body to heal itself. (Sharry Edwards, Sound Health Resources, Hocking College Conference Center, 15600 Wolfe-Bennett Road, Nelsonville, Ohio, 45764, phone: 614-753-3930. Also Elaine Thompson, Vibrational Retraining, The Cottage, 81 West End, Street, Somerset, BA16 OLQ, England, phone: 01458-443794.) We can assist this process by determining which notes we are missing and singing them ourselves. This is what swimming among dolphins does for us. They send out an appropriate balancing note. Our brain waves experience it, accept it and eventually begin to resonate it in our own bodies. Developing our inner hearing and vibrational sensitivity prepares us to heal with our sounds and songs. The quality and purity of our intentions and the health of our physical bodies also impacts the effectiveness of this process.

Before I understood any of this, the dolphins were preparing me by teaching me to make healing sounds. By singing certain frequencies, we can regulate such things as our heart rates, nervous systems, nutrient absorption, and numerous other bodily systems. Rather than doing everything automatically and without awareness, we can take conscious control of these physical processes in the way the dolphins have learned to control their breathing, sleeping, birthing and the physiological pressures of deep diving.

August 19, 1995

Swimming with the dolphins today, I was impressed again by their perseverance and patience. *Lumpy* and *Singer* have been my teachers all week, and my "classes" have included repeated mimicry. Each sound that they make, I repeat as best I can with as accurate a tone as I can sing. Being physically close to them seems to expedite this. I have found that making these same sounds on land is not as effective as immediately mimicking their whistles in the ocean. I have also noticed a change in the way I make sounds. For the first hour as I swim alongside *Lumpy*, I feel as though I am straining my throat. Then a change takes place and I am able to easily make sounds that seem to bypass my vocal cords. The sounds I make resonate in my brain and head. They are very high-pitched. I have also developed my inner ear to an acute level of hearing and sensing. As I imitate *Lumpy* I notice I am over-toning. In my cranium, I hear an echo that is harmonizing with the predominant tone I am sounding. I am enjoying these spontaneous harmonics.

Now the dolphins are beyond my ability to hear and I stop sounding. I hear nothing but the water lapping at my ears. Yet somehow I think they are still sounding, a mile away, still testing my ability to hear and answer them. I hold my body very quiet in the water, hardly breathing, going deeper and deeper into my awareness, listening for the familiar sounds I have come to love. In the silence I experience feelings of well-being that pass through my entire body. I am at peace. I know *Singer* and *Lumpy* will soon be doubling back to swim alongside me again, encouraging me to continue our lessons.

DOLPHINS AND OPERA

As a teenager, I could not carry a tune. My voice was weak and off-key. In school I was placed in the back row of the choir and told not to sing, only mouth the words silently. I rarely sang unless I wanted to be teased. This continued into my adult life — to my frustration, because I loved to sing popular songs but felt too embarrassed to do so. Now, with the dolphins' help, my voice has improved greatly and I am able to sing with clarity and a wide range of notes.

One day after a wonderful cetacean singing class I was immersed in deep waves of love. I shared with the dolphins my wish to bring this experience to other people. How could I reproduce this soothing, satisfying vibration while living on land? The dolphins picked up my thoughts and sonared one word back to me: *Opera.*

Opera? Did I hear that right? Opera. I knew very little about it and never had listened to it with any appreciation. What could they mean? After swimming back to my house, I mentioned this to some visiting friends from Holland, Irena, Lydia and Catherine. Without a word, they drove to the music store and bought me five CDs of opera sopranos. Listening intently to the sounds, I suddenly felt chills move up and down my body as Joan Sutherland, Kathleen Battle and Sheila Armstrong sang notes topping our musical scales. I was filled with deep joy experiencing the beauty of their voices and elated to know that some of the dolphins' sounds could be so melodically duplicated by humans. The dolphins were right, some opera singers were able to hit the same high C's (high seas!) that I recognized among my dolphin teachers.

I began to practice singing opera music (much to the dismay of my neighbors!) Sometimes having to resort to the privacy of long car rides to practice, I found my voice improving in proportion to the joy filling my heart from the pure tones. More than singing the songs, I preferred to focus on certain notes I liked, repeatedly singing them like "Johnny-One-Note," holding the note, pure and true for as long as possible.

SOUND AND SHAPE-SHIFTING

During the period that these dolphin singing lessons were occurring, my interest in understanding and translating dolphin language in regard to these sounds led me to listen to audio tapes I had previously recorded of the dolphins. The Navy had lent me top quality hydrophone equipment for two weeks to record their vocalizations. The dolphins kindly cooperated by showing up every day and being exceptionally vocal.

Listening to these tapes I suddenly noticed something I had not heard before. Certain high-pitched dolphin sounds were followed by complete silence. The tape would be rolling along, many dolphins would be vocalizing, I could hear the sound of the microphone bumping against the side of the kayak, the waves against the cliff, the fish eating the coral, some static — then a singular high-pitched dolphin whistle rang out followed by silence. For a few seconds on the stereo, no other sounds could be heard! Then, shortly, the cacophony of sounds would begin again.

My experience at *Oceansong* bookstore in California flashed into my mind. The high-pitched sound that stopped time! I was being reminded of it again, in my own living room, coming from my own sound system. A wave of recognition rolled over me as I fully understood what the dolphins had been trying to convey.

There are sounds that stop time, that alter reality, that can be used as tools to shift dimensions. They are sounds that prepare us to enter the unknown without fear. My friends and I had been experiencing them as we swam in the water surrounded by the dolphin pods. In fact sometimes the human/dolphin frequencies we echoed were so mind altering that we lost contact with physicality. We were out of body. On occasion the vibrations of our physical matter were so

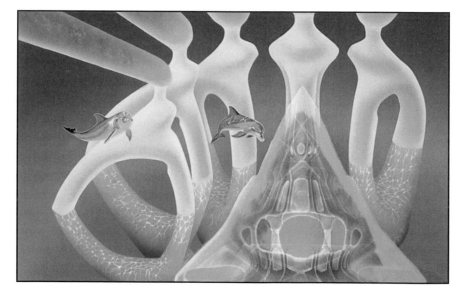

heightened, we became invisible to third-dimensional reality, and people around us could not see us. We could see the higher geometric forms of Beauty created by sound.

These tones can transform all things. They can heal and change our bodies and our environments. They can dematerialize and materialize matter, and even change the physical structure of objects (demonstrated in the third-dimension by sound that can shatter glass). In the fifth-dimensional world "sound-shifting" is a technology for regenerating and reorganizing matter.

SOUND TRANSPORTATION

After this discovery, I became very sensitive to high-pitched sounds in my environment, feeling their effect on my subtle and physical bodies. Along with the sounds of the wonderful opera sopranos, I practiced the sharp, staccato, high-pitched tonal language used by inhabitants of the Pleiades to balance human bodies. I listened to the sounds of Orcas and I sounded in the ocean among the visiting Humpbacks. We exchanged high notes with powerful silences between each harmonic vocalization. I began swimming among the Pilot whales, who also resonate high-frequency whistles. I listened to CDs of the Noh Theater musicians in Japan, who use similar sounds and silences to create altered states of consciousness. I heard the high-pitched frequencies of space ships from the Pleiades that use a tonal propulsion system to enter our atmosphere. All of these sensitive beings use sounds to transport themselves into other realities. In Earth time, a second is all you need to transport yourself into an expanded realm where there are no time restrictions. By shifting our frequencies, we access this other dimension of timelessness. The tones and sonar of the cetaceans align with our frequency waves and through sounds we enter a realm where our perceptions increase as we become aware of a wider range of subtle vibrating objects and beings.

THE POWER OF SOUND CONFERENCE

The subject of Sound as a healing modality and as a frequency to access multiple dimensions has evoked great interest and enthusiasm among spiritually aware people. Sharry Edwards of Sound Health Resources in Ohio, and Barbara Hero, creator of the Lambdoma Harmonic

Keyboard in Maine, wrote to me expressing interest in understanding the dolphins' use of sound. I invited them to Hawaii to meet the dolphins. When I traveled to England with my soul-partner, Dr. John Float, we visited our friend, Elaine, in Glastonbury and as we talked about our mutual work of supplying missing frequencies for people's bodies for their self-reparation, we awakened a deep compassion for this subject, amplified by our triad of energy and our Spiritual Guides. Meditating in the third floor suite of Elaine's Bed and Breakfast Hotel, overlooking the sacred site of the Tor, we called upon the Ascended Masters for guidance. We were shown the vision of a Sound Conference to respond to the outpouring of dedicated interest in the subject of Sound and Health. The idea filled us with so much excitement, we immediately began planning this educational and experiential event. And so the date was set and from June 16-22, 1996 John and I co-facilitated the Power of Sound Conference in Kona, sponsored by the Dolphin Connection, Hawaii. The welcoming letter expressed our intentions: "In our work with the dolphins and whales and their sonar and sonic transmissions, we have been indelibly blueprinted to a new cellular frequency which has inspired us to learn more and more about the power of sound. This has led us over the past months to meetings with remarkable friends who are masters in this field."

The Power of Sound Conference was attended by music and health practitioners from around the world. It was hosted by friends who are inspiring pioneers on the leading edge in this field: Elaine Thompson, Sharry Edwards, Jonathan Goldman, Robert Miller Foulkrod, Jean-Luc Bozzoli, Tim Wheater, Barbara Hero, Chris James, Nancy Gorglione, Elizabeth Eason, Antion and Elandra Meredith; and it ran joyfully and smoothly thanks to the volunteer work of Trish, Doug, Suchi, Nancy, Chris, Debbie, Pomaika'i, James, Inta, Julie, Claudia, Kevin and Jeff.

The Conference gathered talented, multilevel kindred souls who shared their joy and wisdom with each other. The dolphins did not disappoint us. As the entire Conference traveled on boats into the ocean, the dolphin pods joined us in the hundreds and touched everyone with their healing sounds and sonar. We journeyed into other vibratory fields, from deep inside our cells to out-of-body experiences in the spaces beyond. In some of these other spaces, we experienced the vibrating frequencies of advanced geometrical forms as our vehicle of sound travel. The high-pitched tones of the dolphins at our side created a vibrational window through which we passed into other realities. The Joy grew from experiencing these shifts together and our lives were forever impacted by the uplifting affects of sounds that transformed us. John and I are grateful for the music, dance, laughter, inspiring words and openhearted connections that were so freely shared during that week immersed in the Power of Sound and the awakening of Universal Souls.

Antion and Elandra Meredith

7

HOLOGRAPHIC
COMMUNICATION

Yesterday I returned from an extended stay in Bali, Indonesia where I had been swimming with the Common dolphins in the Sea of Java. Both Pods A and B turned out in great numbers today to greet me and my swim partner, Jean-Luc. With great joy, we swam with them for many hours. During those hours they never left our sides, swimming close, touching me and making many sounds. All my favorites were there, including *Exx*, *Zac*, *Ragged Fin*, *Notches*, *Wave*, *Scissors*, *Dimple*, *Three Spot*, *Crater*, *Tippy*, *Old Scar*, *Paint*, *S.A.* (*South America* — has a marking like a map on her right flank), *Baby White Stripes*, *Scooter*, *Sunburst*, and *Remora Kid*. We were filled with so much happiness at this wonderful reunion.

The dolphins were very vocal, making constant sounds of great variety for hours and scanning me with their sonar. I often notice that when I return from a trip the dolphins sonar me more than usual, as if they are able to glean from my body the experiences I have had with dolphins in other locations. In fact, whenever I travel to foreign countries, I visit the captive dolphins in the

Aquariums there, with the thought that they too will be able to access information I carry in my body about swimming in the Pacific Ocean. Assuming that they would enjoy my free-swimming encounters with the Spinner dolphins in the same way I can enjoy a film about wild dolphins, I stand near their tanks and visualize my pods at home.

It also feels as though the dolphins of Pods A and B realign my energy systems that may have been affected by dissonant fields of energy I encounter during flights and travel. When I swam back to shore today, I felt unusually tired and I fell asleep for an hour. When I awoke my head was throbbing. I rarely have headaches, but it seemed that the active sonar from so many dolphins had had a powerful effect on me. The throbbing in my head continued all day as I responded to letters and faxes in my office.

Finally, my friend JoAnn suggested I try a device she had. It was called a Tesla coil, housed in a white cone-shaped case that was about seven inches wide across the base. I lay down in bed and placed it on my third eye, where my head was pounding. Expecting nothing, but glad to lie down and have a rest, I became vaguely aware of a buzzing sensation on my forehead. I then noticed a high-pitched sound that was entering my head from the coil. Focusing my awareness, I was amazed to hear piercing dolphin sounds. Dolphin whistles filled my head. The sounds pulsated along with the headache, until I could not separate the two sensations. It felt as though large quantities of information from the dolphins this morning were congested in my head. Suddenly I saw in my mind's eye an image of the adult dolphins swimming with their babies. As I saw the image, I received a transmission. The dolphins were telling me that they bring the baby dolphins to swim with me because they are teaching their young simultaneously with me, the same information at the same time. I am like a child in their family, a new student in their school of wisdom. The swimming, the spiraling, their sonar and their sounds are conveying information to the brain and the cells of my body in a sonic hologram.

As the sounds of the Tesla coil spiraled into me, the throbbing in my head decreased and I fell into a deep sleep. This information-packed image was the beginning of my studies about dolphin Holographic Communication.

THE CO-CREATION OF COMMUNICATION

Dolphins communicate holographically. Volumes of information enter my awareness with a single holographic transmission from them. The exchange is not linear or two-dimensional, as when people speak to me. Instead, the information the dolphins give me comes with feelings, colors and sounds, past, present and future truisms all at once. I have no questions or need for further clarification. The transmission moves into my consciousness and merges with my existing knowledge.

To explain this concept, I will use an example of a sentence related in a linear way: "The girl plays with a ball in the park." When we hear those words our minds interpret it based on our understanding of parks and girls and playing. Everyone's interpretation will be different. The sentence is also limited in the information it conveys about the girl and her environment. To learn more we would need to ask questions such as, "How old is the girl? What is she wearing? Who else is in the park? Are there trees? Flowers? Pathways? What color is the ball? What time of day is it? What is the weather?" and so on.

In contrast, a dolphin communicating the same information about the girl, would instantly send a visual image with color, feelings, and rich details about every aspect of the projected thoughtform. I would be able to see and feel the green park, the liveliness of the girl's three friends, how old the child is, her bright purple ball, the sun-dappled trees, blue sky, soft breeze, the aroma of honeysuckle, the songs of families of birds. It would feel as though I had been transported to the park. The dolphin's message would be a complete package of information, containing all pertinent data, and could not be misinterpreted.

Linear and holographic methods of communicating can be compared to the differences between an artist's brush and a camera. An artist paints a picture stroke by stroke until eventually an entire picture is revealed. This is linear. A photographer looks at a beautiful landscape and, using her camera, reproduces the image instantly. The picture is captured with one click of her camera. It is as simple and as quick as that. Similarly, the dolphins…Click!…on us and we receive their visual transmission, plus much more!

The new paradigm of communication the dolphins want us to learn gives us the ability to contact each other in this instantaneous way. Some of us are already doing this. For example, we can learn a lot by feeling empathy for a person who is describing something to us, especially when the person is someone we know well. Many nuances and details are revealed by the person's tone of voice, eye contact, feelings, body stance and telepathy. Becoming more aware of our ability to do this enhances this innate skill.

The dolphins also communicate by interacting with thoughtforms. They often imprint their impressions on what I am thinking. Their information seeps into the intelligence of my cells, where I can then access it intellectually. This has led to my asking them directly for information, especially when I have dolphin-related work to do. It is common for me to swim among the pod while focusing on the participants in an upcoming Seminar, and then be filled with the dolphins' ideas about the seminar topics to teach, the attendees' interests, needs and dreams, how to introduce certain topics in a culturally clear way, and even where to bring the participants for their dolphin encounters.

The dolphins and I co-create information by merging our thought patterns and brain waves. We share thoughts that relate to whatever we are thinking and feeling in the present moment. These thoughts are dynamic and have an "emotional charge" as a bioelectric conductor of our energy exchange. Our empathy, or love, is the bioelectric current we each send out. As our currents cross, the dolphin pod and I create a live-wire where our fields of energy merge, resulting in an image or a piece of information, available to us all, that is a product of our mutual interaction. It is a fascinating way to make contact because it is always about communicating in the Now. There are no hidden agendas, no cultural differences, no unclear words or thoughts, no misunderstandings. It is a refreshing way to communicate, and also great fun because the information is often so unexpectedly different than what I would receive on my own in a linear conversation. Their understanding and view of the world through my thoughtforms is wonderfully simple, heartfelt and expansive. I appreciate the dolphins' perspectives and my rational mind is intrigued by the clever truths they bring to Light.

For example, one day I asked the dolphins, "Who in the pod is the leader?" The dolphins transmitted an image of the pod to me. They were all swimming together, and then one of the dolphins in the middle made a sharp turn to the left. At that, all the other dolphins slowly veered left and continued to swim in unison. I was trying to see who the dolphin was that had made the first move so I would know who was "the leader." Then a message came into my awareness from the pod, *We lead from the center. Whoever has the strongest intention in any given moment leads the rest.* Aha! Lead from your "center." Their holographic transmission had answered both my obvious question and my unspoken questions about spiritual leadership.

This is a new paradigm in communication. It is a way of gaining information, beyond rational processing and deductions. It is a type of perception in which we just *Know*. Rather than superficially seeing and hearing each other, we *experience* the vibrations of all the energy forces that are in, or that travel through, people. Other people's vibrations interact directly with our own, and we thus learn about each other through our bodies' physical elements and vibrational forms. The intelligence (or mind) in all of our cells, not our analytical brains, receives information from other beings, making us immediately aware of what they are "saying." The message does not come through as words, but as powerful feelings that impact our physical structure.

For most people, interpreting holographic communication with dolphins will initially rely on an intuitive response, since our speech patterns and their consciousness are so different. Dolphin holographic "language" does not use subjects, verbs and objects as in the English language. When I am receiving information from dolphins a "feeling-tone" of information enters my awareness, my consciousness, my entire body, my heart, all my cells. It interacts and merges with my knowledge, to produce an awareness of our two worlds as one. This is how the dolphins would like us to communicate with them. We send out a thoughtform or image or tone and they do likewise. The two thoughtforms will then merge and co-create a new image. The end result is a fascinating vibrational exchange which is creative and enlightening for both participants.

Can you imagine what it will be like when we all learn to communicate in this way? There will be no more deception and untruth. Everything will be known. Honesty and integrity will prevail. This type of intimate exchange will lead to feelings of closeness and appreciation. When we understand each other this well, our love for each other will grow, and allow us to connect with the Truth of who we are.

This way of communicating is a new way of living which can ultimately heal our planet and bring peace to people. Swimming with dolphins allows us to experience this way of relating and reminds us to live in an environment where we can connect with a collective consciousness of love, wisdom, compassion, reverence and joy. Resonating with the qualities of our basic nature, we feel a return to wholeness when we make the dolphin world our own.

MAINTAINING THE INTEGRITY
OF YOUR CHOSEN WORK

February 18, 1991

It is 6:34 a.m. I feel as though I am still dreaming as I swim out to meet the dolphins. A huge pod appears. As they sweep by me, forgetting all else, I swim away with them. There are at least sixty-two dolphins, and we swim together for two hours. They are energetic as is often the case when large numbers, more than twelve or sixteen, gather together. They are also noisy, using their sonar and making constant whistles and clicks among themselves.

They are whirling and spiraling around each other, a maze of dolphins turning and churning around and whistling loudly. When I join their play and swim upside down and spin, they become excited, spiraling and dancing even more, sonaring me and watching me while never missing a graceful turn. Instinctively I sing and screech with them. I sound more and more like them each day. They come up to meet me and include me in their play. Soon we are all spinning together and I am breathless, but as relentless as they are. I surface for air and dive again as they continue to include me in their weaving dance.

We spend many sessions like this. Occasionally my lungs need a rest and I opt to float silently on top, watching them play. Today as I rest and observe them, I become aware of a message. It is a vision of their community of joy, playing and perhaps working together, enjoying their camaraderie and synchronicity. Then, clearly, *"We merge our energies with each other, but none of us lose ourselves in this merging, we are still individual beings who maintain our autonomy. Remember to hold your space in the midst of chaos and community, in all partnerships and relationships. Do not lose the integrity of who you are and what you represent. Stay true to your chosen path. Be aware and do not compromise yourself."*

The message comes as a distinct feeling, rather than words. I receive it in the way all dolphin communications come to me...as a total piece of information...Zap! Right out of the blue! One minute I am enjoying watching them, the next I am surrounded by a body of information that has a message for me.

As the months after this communication passed I had many opportunities to think about its meaning. With worldwide interest in dolphins increasing, people often approached me about documentaries and articles and photos. Everyone seemed to have a good cause for their projects. Without the dolphins' reminder, I would have been tempted to fill my home with people and activity. But when I allow this, as I occasionally do, I soon have very little time left to continue my research. The dolphins reminded me to hold my space and do what I love. This message was especially helpful for me because my psychological history, typical of many women in our culture, has been one of setting aside my own needs at the request of others. Now I was being reminded to hold on to my dreams and to learn to say "No" to distractions in a kind but definite way. Learning to do this gently, with grace and love, has led to continued joy in my daily life. I ask myself regularly, "Am I having fun today? Am I doing what I love?" We can easily be distracted by temporary projects, busy work and getting overly involved in the work of others. It's up to us to stay true to ourselves and our paths to insure fulfilling lives. No one else can do this for us. When we respect our own needs, everyone benefits along with us and the world becomes a better place.

KNOWING WHO WE ARE...OUR EVOLUTION

Knowing and honoring who we are is an important aspect of our personal growth towards love of self and our Earth. When asking the dolphins for suggestions about my own spiritual path and evolution and how to experience it fully, I received guidance about the importance of mastering three concepts.

To assist in our evolution, it is important to know ourselves: who we are, what we are made of, where we came from, and why we are here. The quest for self-knowledge is as old as life itself. It is the most important tenet of the world's great books of wisdom: "Know thyself and to thine own self be true." Currently, *Human Psychology* is a favorite course of study at universities. We learn about ourselves through meditation, counseling and self-awareness books and workshops. We seek reasons for existing at this time, in this space, and we are working through lessons that enhance our spiritual growth.

In our growing awareness, we are identifying ourselves as beings who value Love above all else, and we are confirming our belief in Love by changing our lifestyles accordingly. We are coming to know ourselves as vibrations of Love, and in so doing we are beginning to understand ourselves and our world in a new light. Instead of feeling alienated we are accepting the Oneness of all life. This is a "requirement" for entrance into the fourth dimension, and is certainly a vital attribute to develop. For if we truly know ourselves, we have the connection with Universal Love which makes all things available to us.

The second important concept that assists in our evolution is learning to control our environment. At first I wondered what that meant…"controlling the environment." I had heard stories that American Indians could speak through the spirit of the mountains and control the weather, and that Hawaiian kahunas could erect stone buildings through a process of levitating boulders. But rather than controlling, these seemed more like working with the environment, assisting the nature spirits and the Mana. The word "control" puzzled me because I related it to people's desire to control their environment in a way that was manipulative, unnatural and unhealthy for Earth. I thought it was better to learn to respect and listen to our environment.

Swimming with the dolphins helped me to understand a different meaning of the concept of *control*. They conveyed to me that we affect our environment and the people around us with our attitudes and feelings. We tend to allow feelings to leave our bodies without awareness of their impact. But people, animals and plants are often easily affected by our state of mind, our sadness or joy. If our friends feel as we do, we assume their sensitivity to our feelings and their ability to read our minds is an indicator of how much they love us. We may feel hurt if they seem unaware of what we are experiencing, even though we may not have explained ourselves to them. We expect people who know us and love us to understand our feelings and intuit our needs.

I then clearly saw that the idea that we affect our environment directly relates to our ability to create our own reality. We are doing this, whether we are aware of it or not. The vibrations we send out attract similar vibrations to us. It's a law of physics and metaphysics: *like attracts like.* We can attract either inspiring or limiting life events, according to our ability to release or hold on to old beliefs and habits. Once we take responsibility for our emotions, thoughts, bodies and spiritual vibrations — once we take control of them — we see that we do indeed create our reality and have control over our own environment. Our loving thoughts and behaviors can have a positive effect on the people around us, on nature and animals, on our community, our country and our planet. It is time to use the power of Love that we all possess in a helpful, directed and compelling way. That is why we are here.

How does the concept of "intentional evolution" allow for the experience of "going with the flow?" Do we really want to control anything? Ideally all of Earth's life forms are compatible with each other, giving and receiving as a part of the whole, flowing within a natural rhythm. This is certainly one of our spiritual objectives, an ideal state to attain. However, unless we take responsibility for what is happening in our own lives and worldwide right now, it could take us a while to reach that level of Oneness with Universal Mind. We are not separate from the collective consciousness. Whether we acknowledge it or not we are part of the energy system that creates reality on Earth. By being mindful of the energy expressions we send out, we can make it a better place.

The third essential concept for spiritual advancement is to recognize and develop our connection to the cosmos and to life beyond the third dimension. We are not alone in the Universe. There are billions of other planets and many of them have life forms that are simply not visible to our three-dimensional eyes or detectable with our three-dimensional technologies. But we can connect with these other planetarians energetically and benefit from their knowledge. Civilizations which are a mere three hundred years ahead of our own have advanced technologies and wisdom beyond our imagination. As we increase our harmonic vibrational frequencies, through meditation, the arts, and being in Love, we will enter dimensions beyond the third. There are aspects of ourselves that exist in parallel realities and energy fields beyond our awareness. The dolphins interact with these other planes of existence and even reside within other dimensions in the ocean. As masters of cosmic travel, they are teaching us their wisdom of Universal Oneness. They are aware of their intrinsic connections to the magnetic streams of energy from other entities, stars and planets and are inviting us to open our belief systems to multiple realities.

DOLPHIN COMMUNICATION SPHERES

The dolphins were teaching me many things about life. The lessons usually came during periods of play in the water. As we dove and spiraled together underwater, a hologram of information would suddenly enter my awareness. It seemed to surround me when I was least expecting it, while I was concentrating on mimicking their behavior or learning from them. Often the hologram was preceded by a barely perceptible sensation in my body that felt like a change in the vibratory field within and around me. This served as a signal to me that something was being sent. I was aware of a spherical energy bubble encompassing me and becoming a receptacle for receiving information from the dolphins. When my mind was quiet, and often when I was physically preoccupied or meditatively relaxed, the subtle sphere would surround me and the dolphin communications ensued.

Now it is time for all of us to practice this method of communication and use it to send information intentionally to other life forms on and off the planet. When we contact the essence of our spiritual selves, the vibration of who we truly are, we emit a vibration that radiates directly with the spiritual essence of other beings. When our essences vibrate at the same frequency, we can merge. Many things can then be transmitted. Our essence is a vibratory sound wave system that moves naturally through space. When we are open to our environment, we easily access information. We ask a question and the answer immediately comes to us because it already exists somewhere in the ethers. If I wonder why the dolphins have not come to play today, and I remain in a listening mode, the answer will quickly enter my awareness. It is that simple. As we practice it, our ability to communicate in this way will grow stronger.

As a species, we are evolving into the fourth dimension and beyond. The Earth is making a massive shift and we are riding along with her! As we learn to expand our energy fields into the next dimension, we will change our perceptual and physical world. We will take control of our reality and be co-creators of many others. In one vision the dolphins showed me a sister planet of our Earth that has been replicated holographically. This twin planet has all the positive attributes of Earth and is without pollution, war and greed. We can shift into this parallel world at will and may very well do so when Earth-changes occur. It is a refined holographic field, a product of higher dimensions, that we are co-creating now. The dolphins are preparing us for this field, by playfully shifting realities in the ocean and communicating with us holographically. It is time for the human race to make the transition to higher consciousness and join the multitude of beings who reside there already. As soon as there is a critical mass of Earth people who can transcend the third dimension, we will be there!

PARTICIPATORY RESEARCH

My way of being with the dolphins is as a researcher who lives among them to learn about their culture. Overall I choose not to label the work I am doing with the dolphins, because sometimes labeling an activity immediately limits our understanding of that process. But over time, the name "Participatory Research" has come to effectively express the nature of my interactive dolphin communication research. This work is quite different from traditional types of observational and experimental research conducted on dolphins. Participatory Research requires that the scientist participate *with* the dolphins and whales in the educational process. It does not separate the human from the cetacean as the observer and the observed. As I collect information, there is no division between researcher and subject, teacher and student, their physical body and mine, their energy field and mine. We are connected by our close proximity to each other, by our awareness of each other and by the frequencies that move life through our bodies. Our information merges to co-create a unity of mind, feelings and wave patterns. We influence each other, we affect each other and we both benefit from this energy exchange.

When a dolphin swims towards me, I move into a parallel position alongside her and join her as any other dolphin would. I open myself empathically to the feelings and thoughts I receive in her presence. But I do not just passively register these, I also respond back to her, understanding that my response to her is as significant as her original communication to me. The research is about the interaction we share with each other. To accomplish this, it is important that I remain open to the unexpected, treat each exchange as unique, and resist any inclination to apply previously made interpretations to the interactions. The dolphins support this by continually changing their behavior. The minute I think, "Aha, I see a pattern in their interactions with me; I know what's coming next," they behave in a way that is different from anything they have done before. This experience encourages me to accept reality as constant change and spontaneity, and to live in the present without depending on unnecessary beliefs from the past. This freedom from old behaviors and beliefs is rare in human societies, however, it predominates in another civilization with which I interact. This will be explained more fully in the following chapters about ETs.

JOINING THE FAMILY

Participatory Research requires perseverance and stamina. It means swimming with dolphins on a daily basis and mimicking their behavior and sounds. It is similar to the way a baby learns to be a part of her family and society — she is silent at first, strengthening her eyes and ears, observing and listening. Gradually she imitates sounds and behaviors from her environment as she learns about life in her family. I am doing the same with my dolphin family. I am learning about them and about living in the ocean. It is a different way of life, a different dimension which includes ways of communicating more advanced than those we use on land.

The dolphins are preparing us for contacts with ETs by demonstrating how we can merge our fields of energy with each other and not feel threatened. When you are willing to disclose the fullness of who you are to other life forms, you will enjoy an inspiring and dynamic exchange of wisdom. But if you reject the communication by trying to shut down, by analyzing it with three-dimensional interpretations, or by choosing fear, your exchange will reflect those fears instead of Love. You draw to yourself the feelings that you are emoting. Will you choose fear or love? With the dolphins I always choose love and so my interactions are joyful. We have the same choice when communicating with ETs — with the Nordics, the Greys and the Golden Ones, the Arcturians, the Sirians, the Pleiadians, the Orions, the Martians — *all* planetary beings. They all communicate through mind-merging, and it is a very pleasant and clear form of expression. Communicating with other beings in this way affects my feelings and thoughts and spiritual essence — it reminds me of being with the whales.

December 5, 1993

A kayak is approaching as the dolphins pull a little further away from me in the water, and I stop to look up. From the amount of gear strapped to their little boat, I decide they are tourists. I guess they have been observing me, because when I wave a greeting, the woman asks me if the dolphins let me touch them. "Oh no," I say, "the dolphins don't like you to touch them when you're just getting to know them. It wouldn't be polite." She nods in understanding.

"Are they always here?" she asks me.

"No. Before today, they haven't been here for a week. I think they are busy communicating with the whales who will be arriving soon from Alaska."

"The whales!!! Do they come into this bay? When will they be here?" she queries.

"Soon." I reply.

"Do you mean this afternoon?" she says.

But the dolphins have returned to play and I never answer her question. I laugh to myself hearing her voice echoing in my mind. "This afternoon!" I have been feeling the approaching whales. Their thoughts are on my mind. Other friends who swim regularly in these dolphin waters have been sensing the whales too. We must be receiving their long-distance holographic communications at subtle levels. But they aren't due on this part of the island for another month.

Now Pod C is all around me again, weaving in a rambunctious and splashy manner, pushing against me mindlessly in their nipping games with each other. I turn my attention back to them as we all dive together, on our sides, angling toward the bottom. I respond to their whistles by making sounds through my snorkel underwater and releasing a barrage of bubbles at the same time. The dolphins release some too, and I change direction to swim through their bubbles, letting the larger ones break on my solar plexus. As I listen to their next series of whistles and clicks, I hear something different and it takes me only a second to realize what I have heard.

That is not a dolphin sound. It is similar. It is a high-pitched whistle, but it continues on with a series of staccato shrieks, followed by a low groan. Breathlessly I dive and listen again. Sure enough, there it is...now...the wail of a siren, followed by the familiar whoop, whoop, whoop sound. The music of the Humpback whales!

They're here!!! The whales have arrived. I dive and listen again, feeling elated...filled with inexplicable excitement. What a joyous occasion! I dive over and over again, holding my breath, keeping my body quiet to hear the deep, spellbinding resonance of their songs, listening to determine where they are, how far away, how close, how many? It is hard to know because although I hear many different sounds I know that one whale can make many tones simultaneously. Is it one whale or many?

I swim toward their sound, heading into the open ocean, unable to resist their call. "I am on my way! I am so happy you are here. I love you. Wait for me!"

Suddenly I have immense energy. I swim fast and steadily, mindful of distant sounds of approaching boats which wouldn't expect to meet swimmers out here. After swimming a mile, diving and fluking under water for most of it, I can hear how much closer the shrieks and sighs are. I am closer. I can tell by their music. Their beautiful harmonic choruses reverberate across the ocean and into my body.

They are crooning: *"We are One, we know you, we know you dear Friend."*

I empathically respond, "Welcome to Hawaii, welcome to our bay, welcome home. How wonderful that you have come early."

I know these waters so well now, the subtleties, colors, movements and patterns. As I swim, my eyes concentrate on the unending blueness below me. At this time of year, only the adult whales are here and they can remain underwater for a long time. Next month when the whales give birth, they will spend more time on the surface with the young ones who need to breathe more often. My eyes search for their dark shapes in the deep water.

I mimic their far-ranging sounds. Through my snorkel I sound like a fog horn, long and low like the tone of a Hawaiian conch shell, echoing into the emptiness. Will they respond? My heart skips a beat as I see a subtle strip of lighter blue. Can it be the whale's white pectoral fin? Or a shark? Or a dolphin? Something is there. I listen for the next sound. It is piercing, vibrating my bones. I strain my eyes, searching for a familiar shape. Dimly, then clearly, I see a dark form below, filling my view. Am I seeing it or not? I refocus my eyes. Yes! There it is, in the murky blue waters.

Hardly breathing, I silently dive. A huge Humpback whale with bright white coloring on the under side of his slowly moving pectoral fin is lifting his massive head toward me. They have found me! Here in this big ocean, the whales have made contact. I am filled with great love. The whale is frozen in time and space far below me, his form taking shape. He is floating silently upward toward me. His darkness is silhouetted against the blue water below and the light from the sun's rays above. Now his entire body is in sight. Nothing seems to be moving. A breathless moment...Then I see the form of a second whale coming behind him. Two whales! I hardly breathe as I float above in wonder and awe. Like silent ships they move past me, looking at me with their deep, dark-brown eyes. I am motionless, floating in their wake. Then, without seeing how it happens, they pass me by and merge back into the depths of blue blackness. I strain my eyes to see them. They are gone, like a dream, they disappear. I blink and focus and dive...only blue water.

"Thank you for being here and filling me with a deep longing, a deep memory. Thank you for that haunting vision of great serenity that I know will remain with me forever."

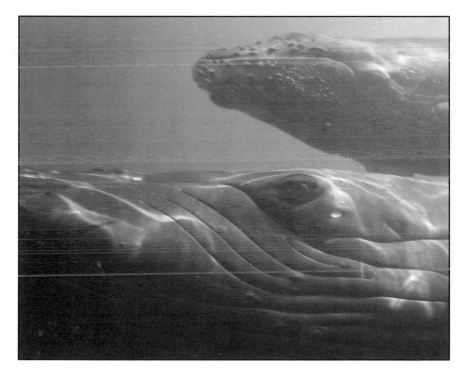

COMMUNICATING WITH WHALES

The whales communicate with me differently than the dolphins. It is easier for me to relate to the dolphins, because they have bodies close in size to my own, they swim easily side by side with me, and I can dive and mimic them. We maintain eye contact and we learn about each other through that contact. They have a twinkle in their eyes that often seems to say, "Let's play!" When I reach out my thoughts, like tendrils from my brain to the dolphins', I feel I am making contact with an intelligence similar to my own. I can send out an impulse that is compatible with their frequency to establish a connection. We communicate using a mind-cell overlap like two loving octopus tentacles intertwining. This is how it feels to me.

With the whales it is different. I reach out the tentacle from my brain and as I grope around in their great unknown, I find nothing — nothing I can latch on to, nothing I can relate to and bring home to my own mind as an information channel, nothing to spark a bioelectric wave for transmission. I reach out, I grope around, I search, and finally I give up.

"That's not it. We do not communicate in that way. Just listen, just be still, just Be."

I relax into the silence. I become aware of a huge all-encompassing cloud of blissful emptiness. Allowing it in, I am lost. There is no more Me. There are no thoughts, no body, no ocean, no Joan. I am submerged in a state of sublime peace that defies definition. My mind is silent, even useless. Never have I felt this before. I want to stay in this gentle and profound state forever. A supreme state of Oneness. This is communication with the whales.

Meeting the Sperm Whale
March 9, 1992

A golden egg-shaped dome of thick light encloses the area as our ship drifts silently in the Sea of Cortez. At first there is one sighting of a Sperm whale spout, the typical side-angled spray from the whale's blowhole on her left side. I watch its cloud-like mist dissolve into the white sky in the distance. It is my first encounter with the mighty Sperm whale, and my heart races with anticipation as I focus my full attention on the distant blue water, now empty and stretching endlessly.

"Dear Sperm Whale, I have longed to meet you. Will I see you close to me? Thank you for being here." Another spray wafts above the water, closer now, and our ship approaches it. There she is, still on the surface. I am within three hundred feet, and I hear the powerful and yet reassuring sound of her breath as she explosively flushes spume from her blowhole. Amid her own churning waves she dives and is gone for ten minutes. I wait, scanning the horizon. My eyes look for her floating dark form among the whitecaps, but my mind goes with her as she dives. I feel the bubbles of air and water caressing her skin. I feel the ease and grace of her plummeting descent, deep into the liquid environment. So big, so solemn, so blue all around. Our minds meet. Nothing...NO things...I am encompassed by a thick cloud, unfamiliar with any of its contents. My mind feels the emptiness. Am I being submerged into alien brainwash? I search my senses for an incoming thought or image. Nothing. I am lost.

Now she surfaces next to me in the frigid water. "I am as close to you as I can possibly get, pressed against the bulkhead of the ship. Only the metal boat walls stand between us. I am content to be where I am, to see you as you spout and cruise near me.

"But now I am being pulled into your cloud-field again. I see you and hear you, but I know nothing. I am surrounded by your essence. All of the material world has disappeared. I am with you again in white darkness."

It feels more familiar now. I allow it. I give up searching for a thought to latch on to, and I sink into it. Ahhhh, a feeling...I am aware of a cocoon of comfort. Sinking into it, I sense a great wisdom melting into me. "What is it?"...No answers.

"Dear Sperm Whale, you have filled me with your essence. Your spirit renews me, your wisdom is beyond words."

In my dreams I meet the whales who are the molecular librarians of Earth's evolution. What we call the Akashic Records lives in the oceans of planet Earth, contained in the water molecules, where information is stored. Since water is never destroyed, only recycled, all of Earth's history remains safe in these ocean archives. The whales can access the information, circulate it and contribute to it — communicating by contacting the intelligence in the water molecules which enter matter and travel through it. As a medical tool, body-fluid analysis of human systems will eventually provide flawless individualized treatment for people's health maladies.

MAKIA IKE KALA

While engaging in Participatory Research, the walls between myself and the cetaceans are transcended. I am immersed in a learning process that uses all of my senses, even the extrasensory perceptions of my skin, vibrational fields, inner ears and eyes, cellular receptors, and my cosmic heritage. Rather than gathering intellectual data, I am gaining information from the whales and dolphins that bypasses my programmed rational mind, allowing information to seep directly into the receptors of my body. It is a process, an unfolding, and we are co-creators of it via one body consciousness to another. It is a perpetual transformative interaction. Imagine our lives when we no longer observe the world as funneled through our five senses, but are instead constantly intimately involved, immersed, incorporated in it.

Not only in our own bodies, but in all matter there is a consciousness that responds to the energy within other matter. Participating with that other consciousness allows the "needs" of both to be fulfilled. When I become a part of this all-encompassing consciousness, this renewed search (research) for the connection with the divine source, my needs are realized through my sincere intentions and compassion. Everything in the universe supports the fulfillment of anything that vibrates in the resonance of Love. My Hawaiian neighbors have a saying: "Makia ike kala," which means, "Energy goes where attention flows. The world is what you think it is. There are no limits."

This is what I feel the dolphins experience. They live this way all the time and so can we. We are truly able to BE in all things. With instantaneous knowing, we can communicate everything in our bodies, our environment, and our universe. We can choose what we attract to ourselves and we can choose what we send out.

The dolphins play with the energies they attract. Maybe they are playing with past, future and parallel lives, with fourth-dimensional ghosts, the energies of the cetaceans in the Arctic, the inner earth, human auric fields, colorful rainbows, or music or entities living on other planets. They can access it all. What a fun way to live! No wonder they seem so joyful. They choose their environment and have total personal control over it. We can too, as you will see in Chapter 11: You Are The Light.

For many years I have been aware of this method of communicating, and have spent a decade encouraging people to swim among the dolphins, to personally experience participatory communication with dolphins and then take it home and continue to practice it among people. In Hawaii I conduct week-long Seminars to assist people in experiencing this advanced method of cellular and soul communication. We already have the skills needed to do this, we merely need to expand our belief systems and practice interspecies and holographic knowing. While swimming and communicating with the dolphins and whales in Hawaii, we remember the fullness of who we really are and we experience the Joy of Union.

Talking Story With Humpbacks
March 24, 1992

Saskia and Krista see some whales on the horizon and they decide to kayak out. I swim out leisurely, seeing nothing but beautiful blue water on the horizon. It is calm, the sky is cloudy. After I pass the *Hana-Like* fishing boat, moored in mid-bay, I stop a moment to look up from the ocean below and there before my eyes is the rounded, black back of a whale! My heart skips a beat as I continue to swim forward. The whale is a large female Humpback mother, with baby. I can see both their backs above the surface momentarily. Now they have turned and are swimming slowly toward me. All is quiet as they disappear beneath the surface. Suddenly deep below I see a strip of bright white. As they continue to move upward toward me I see it is the baby's pectoral fin and right above her is her mother. They swim in front of me side by side and I am awed by their beauty and their fluid motion.

Time seems to stand still as they slowly pass by, the alternate fluking of their tails moving them ahead in perfect synergism. Softly giving thanks, I am moved with emotion at the peacefulness of their passage. The baby is quite small for this late in the birthing season, less than one third the size of the mother. I watch until every detail, every movement of their massive bodies, disappears and even the black darkness of their forms is gone. Then I float in the water, reveling in the beauty of the experience. I am quiet and filled with gratitude.

Now they surface and spout on my left side. I turn to watch them as they roll forward and are out of sight again. How loud the spout is! A powerful explosion of air. No one else is around, not a boat or a swimmer. I am alone with them and acutely aware of their close proximity in the water. I feel no fear, only openhearted love and deep peace. Now I watch as a large tail above the surface gently slips into the water, indicating a shallow dive.

Although they are probably three hundred feet away by now, I dive also, a distant participant in their dance. Perhaps they will sense me. Perhaps they will read me better when I am totally submerged as they are. All is blue, endless blue. I slowly surface and float. They are making no audible sounds. I hear only the lapping of gentle waves on my ears. Remaining in place, I relive the picture of them passing before me. Then I see them again, swimming toward me on the surface, huge masses of wet black. I wait as they slowly dive. In a few seconds they have reached me underwater. I float, watching, hardly breathing. Slowly they move directly beneath me. The mother stops. I realize I've never seen whales *stop* before. But they stop. The mother's body is positioned directly under me, the young one at a right angle to her, with her head hidden under the mother's jaw and forward of the pectoral fin. They remain there in total quiet.

Is the baby sleeping? I think of bedtime stories and I begin to tell them. Stories about all the whales I have recently seen in the Sea of Cortez. Having returned just two days ago, the images are vivid in my mind. I explain my happiness at meeting the Sperm whales and how amazed I am by the unending length of the Blue whales. Then I am silent, listening to the whale's reply. It comes as a wave of emotion. I feel the mother whale's love for her baby and a feeling of great compassion warms my body.

I explain that I understand the love between them because of my newborn grandson. I tell them all about Nathaniel, just born this January in California, and what it feels like to hold him in my arms, close to my heart and look at the miracle of his tiny face. They understand and they listen attentively. For one hour we float together.

During that time, the baby floats up toward me and stays on the surface for a while taking a few breaths. Then she returns to the same place with only her head hidden under her mother's jaw...like a child who covers her eyes and thinks no one can see her. When she surfaces again, she swims next to me. I am thrilled and I cast a quick glance at Mom to make sure this is okay with her. She does not move, so I focus on the little one. She already has barnacles and some scratches on her flank. How did she get those? The baby does an easy half dive next to me, and I respond by diving down with her. She reacts to me by surfacing and diving again. I take a breath, check Mom again and dive alongside.

Now we are playing together. This is a first. I've done it with dolphins, but never with a Humpback whale baby. Coming up again, the youngster stays on the surface. I am looking into her eye. She is definitely checking me out! We stay together side by side before she dives down to Mom again and assumes the same partially hidden position.

The sun has remained behind a cloud and the water is cool. I become aware that my entire body is shaking with cold. The slight current is moving me to the right of the whales. The mother, aware of my shivering, makes a pass by, looking directly into my eyes before moving slowly toward the exit from the bay into the ocean. The baby dawdles with me until the mother surfaces just forty feet from me and does a fluke lob three times on the surface. It is powerfully loud. The young one responds correctly (as she must do when they are traveling long distances), she swims to her mom's side. Now, just fifty feet away, they spout side by side. Watching them, my heart swells with love. And with amazement I watch as they turn back towards me, picking up a fast pace! Coming close to me, they spout together, within touching distance...so loud. Then diving shallowly, just below the surface, they sweep around me, leaving me spinning in the whirling center of their circle. Surrounding me with a complete ring of fluke prints, the flat spaces where the water is motionless from the suction of their descending tails, they head for the open sea. I am pulled into the backwash of their activity, spiraling in their oceanic waves. I understand that they are telling me good-bye for now and that they are acknowledging my presence and my friendship. "Thanks dear friends, for spending an afternoon with me. My love is with you, until we meet again."

9

SHIFTING DIMENSIONS

In 1988 my partner, Jean-Luc, and I decided to stop traveling and settle down for a while to write and paint. I received guidance from a spiritual Light Being, named Arcturus, to move to Hawaii where I would make physical contact with extraterrestrials. Apparently a setting such as the Hawaiian Islands, separated from large land masses and surrounded by water, is an optimum location for ETs to manifest into three-dimensional, physical form.

ETs OF THE OCEAN AND HYPERSPACE

When I met the Spinner dolphins, I wondered if these were the ETs that Arcturus had referred to. I reasoned, "The dolphins don't live on terra firma, the earth, they live in the ocean, so they are 'extra' terrestrial. Could this be what the message from Arcturus meant?" In time I learned that this was indeed part of the plan, but there was still more to come.

My next communication from Arcturus indicated that 1993 was the year the physical contact in Hawaii would occur, and when I mentioned this to my English friend, Elaine, she surprised me by confiding that she had received the same message. She flew to Hawaii and we found a quiet place to enter deep meditation together.

Numerically, 1993 is a "twenty-two" year — meaning if you add the numbers 1 and 9 and 9 and 3 together they equal twenty-two. In my life, major energy and occupational shifts have occurred in the years that total twenty-two. They occur every *nine* years (as in The Nine from Sirius!) For example, in 1984 I met the dolphins for the first time through contact with Jean-Luc, and began my dolphin communication work. In 1975 I had an out-of-body experience in which I remembered my spiritual purposes for this lifetime and began a new path to fulfill them, leaving my old life behind.

So here we were, my friend Elaine and I meditating in the silent seclusion of my spacious bedroom at Dolphin House. Immersing ourselves in Love, we asked that the contact be made. We stated our wish to have "physical" contact, and made a request to board the visiting entities' space vehicle and to retain a conscious memory of it. We requested physical and spiritual healing, along with direction for the next phase of our Earthly work as planetary mediators. We also asked for an increase in our frequencies to the highest level our physical and bioelectrical systems could healthily accept. All of these requests were honored.

Our vibrational frequencies were uplifted and our space friends' frequencies were slowed down to ensure a compatible energy field. Now we could see each other, sit in circle together and telepathically communicate while sharing a common space in time.

A torrent of information infused my awareness with an understanding of my multidimensional connection to Elaine. The information indicated that we would work together, that we were meant to reconnect at this time, and that Glastonbury and Hawaii have connecting ley lines that were currently being activated and reinforced.

We were brought aboard an Arcturian ship and given a tour. My first sensation was that of heat, the result of merging with a high-frequency energy system. It felt as though my skin were moving and different parts of my body were having spontaneous energy spasms. My body seemed to lose physical boundaries and felt as though it were wavy. I realized that perfect physical health is the optimum circumstance for this dematerialization process. I felt heat and pressure on my lungs and solar plexus.

Aboard the ship I found myself in a tubular chamber filled with lights and sounds, which prepared my energy system for the frequencies on the ship. The ship was huge. I was taken on a tour by a small group of Space Friends who were robed and bright. Their faces were radiant, and I realized that facial features such as ours are less important when communicating telepathically, mind to mind (and group mind at that). During the tour of the ship I saw the following rooms:

A room with seats enclosed in bubbles that ensured people vibrated at the appropriate frequency when visiting different resonant realities. The bubble-seats changed the occupant's vibrations.

A room like a cafeteria with many small cubicles in the walls. However, these were not filled with food. They were energy rejuvenation sockets. Beings came into the room with "assignments" coded on computer chips. They inserted these chips into the cubicles, holding on to the ends, and were filled with the forces needed to balance their energies, revive them or convert them for their next assignment on Earth or elsewhere.

A room where "scout ships" were docked and prepared for launching, with many mechanics working on large technical equipment built into the walls. These smaller scout ships were for going into Earth's atmosphere and gleaning information about the social life on Earth and the progress of Earthlings. They would bring the information back to the mother ship. They were made of an amazing type of fluid construction which allowed them to expand large or contract small as needed for a particular mission. Sometimes they darted around as very small disks, sometimes they enlarged themselves to bring people aboard in physical form.

A room with many beams of Light that constantly moved about, like search lights crisscrossing each other. Although they communicated the purpose of the room to me with imagery and thoughts, I still could not understand exactly what it was — it may have been propulsion.

A room in which there were large glass cubicles in the wall that appeared to contain bodies or inanimate physical forms. It seemed to be a place where different body types could be activated as needed. It was also a resting place for passengers using the ship to travel long distances to different solar systems. When traveling for Light Years the concept of Time is no longer relevant, so these beings traveled on this ship and waited until the ship's work on Earth, or wherever, was completed before being brought to their destinations. Some of these beings were waiting to be of service on Earth, but would disembark only when the cosmic timetable and escalating frequencies on Earth were appropriate for their enlightening energy work. In looking at this room I realized it was the kind of place that some Earth people would have difficulty understanding and accepting because it was beyond society's present view of the potentials and versatility of our physical bodies. Without an understanding that our physical selves are receptacles for our spirits *by choice*, a reality that normalizes living out-of-body is still a radical idea for most humans. This viewpoint has kept many people from being invited aboard space ships because the ETs do not want to upset us; much of the advanced technology there would be misconstrued by a third-dimensional view of life.

A control room with tables whose surfaces were huge screens revealing Earth and the cosmos and whose walls were filled with illuminated plaques and colorfully lighted, two inch squares. The beings there worked silently and efficiently. It looked very familiar to me. I realized I had worked in that part of the Ship many times before, without consciously recalling it back on Earth.

Elaine's experience was of entering the Ship and seeing clearly the robed forms and radiant faces of the people. She also saw a *huge* pool with dolphin emissaries in it and upright dolphinoid ETs around it. She saw a room where forms became energy and flowed among each other within air currents of colors and sounds. This room was for cleansing vibrational fields after sojourns to other planets, as well as a play area for energies to merge with each other and enjoy the beauty of that unique freedom of formlessness. Elaine has drawn images of the ship's crew of Light Beings and is publishing them in a book, sharing her experiences about new realities and multiple life forms beyond our three-dimensional Earth ones.

I was shown that in the years ahead, human beings would acknowledge the presence of Space Beings and would seek guidance from qualified people to explain the phenomena to them. Many people are now preparing for that role by communicating with dolphins.

Part of the cosmic help being extended to our planet by our space friends is that of acclimating people to multiple frequencies and helping them access numerous dimensions the way dolphins and whales do. Why is this important? I have seen images of astrophysical changes in the cosmos that are occurring now in our Milky Way galaxy.

Our solar system is moving into a new band of energy. Earth's vibrations will be increased as a result of these changes. It is a wonderful process of development that is a natural part of the evolution of our galaxy. It is helpful to be aware that Earth's resonant frequency is gradually increasing and to feel it affecting our emotional, physical and mental bodies, to be aware of our heightened intuition and precognitions. Physical Earth changes lead to cellular changes in all physical matter incarnated on the planet, and as part of the physical matter of Earth, our bodies are trying to match the Earth's shifting frequency. Illnesses in our bodies are reflected in the weather patterns and geochemistry of the Earth. Our thoughts take on more and more "weight" as Earth's spiritual frequencies increase and matter becomes lighter. We can choose to use our Group Mind like the dolphins to attain planetary consciousness and spiritually evolve, or we can stay within our present belief systems and remain as we are. Earth will go through her changes regardless.

Everything on Earth is already starting to move faster. Have you noticed that? You may feel tired and experience physical illness as your cells change. Do not worry about this. Take good care of yourself, be loving and kind. Perhaps you have noticed that you are more forgetful as you release your attachment to past memories and begin to live in the present moment. You may not remember what day it is or what you had for dinner last night or the name of your best friend! This is because you are removing from your reality information that no longer serves you in the moment. In this transition process, different pieces of information are floating in and out and may get "lost."

Your reasoning mental self may feel confused when your former, practical solutions for problem-solving don't work anymore. You are being asked to trust the voice of your heart in making decisions. Your rational self is now in equal partnership with your heart and feelings. Your faith in yourself to make decisions based on *love* is being called forth. Earth's new frequencies support inner knowing and intuition. Our perceptions are being expanded due to the new band of Light surrounding Earth.

By letting our thoughts and our vibrational memories resonate with certain geometric frequencies, we can learn how to shape-shift our forms and how to be whole. So think positively and align yourself with the Light, for as the Universe changes and evolves, so do we. We are inseparable from the sacred geometric forms of Creation and the energy fields they generate within our bodies, the planet, and on out into the matrices of the universe. The biophysical aspects of our species have evolved and now we are progressing towards the evolution of our consciousness and our super-mind.

EMOTIONAL ROLLER-COASTERS

Remember, emotions are vibrations. Allow your emotions to evolve you. Appreciate them, because it is your feelings and emotions that are transmuting your DNA.

However do not get caught up in these emotions and allow them to direct your life, just let them pass through you. You will experience many emotions as your heart and feelings become more dominant. Make decisions based on love, asking yourself, "What is the most loving choice I can make right now?" It's important not to make decisions based on an emotional upsurge or downsurge. Your emotions are not good barometers of what is actually happening in your psyche, because they are often connected to your ego needs. Be your own witness and observe your personal melodrama, but don't be ruled by it. Let the feelings from your heart and your intellect guide you, not your uncontrolled emotions. As The Nine from Sirius once told me regarding these times of change, "Observe the ripples and surf the wave."

This type of change has never happened in all the history of the Earth and now it is happening with over six billion people on board! As the frequencies of the Earth increase, our cells are trying to keep up and resonate with it. However, our physical matter may be having difficulty doing this because our beliefs are holding us back. Everything on Earth is changing. The rocks, the trees, and the animals are all shifting naturally into a higher frequency. We could be experiencing these evolutionary shifts right along with them, except that the strong energy fields created by our belief systems and our fears are blocking our vibrational progress. Ironically, most of our fears are unfounded and will never materialize. It's good to recognize that many of them are inherited beliefs from our relatives and society, that we can now reject. We will experience that which we identify with, and that which we have any emotional charge about will be drawn to us. When we move away from old belief systems, we will resonate instead with new bodies of information. Become aware of your love for the earth and let that love expand your field of energy. Your heart will facilitate your transformation.

The words we use in our everyday conversations become prophetic. Within the new, high-frequencies of Light, our words carry a vibrational tone that has a lot of weight and will manifest into physical form more quickly than ever. So become mindful of pessimistic, derogatory words and ideas you express. They can create a reality you do not want.

It is important to identify with the highest good and the most angelic beings. Focusing on the loving energies of the dolphins and other enlightened souls nurtures our spirits. We are never made to experience processes that are too difficult for us. We have the tools we need to accept the challenges and benefit from them. Even the upcoming geophysical changes are within our abilities to influence and evolve through. We are developing new capabilities in the neurological circuits in our brains. New physical elements are being activated. When we remain centered in Love and Light, surround ourselves in Peace, and expand our willingness to Trust in the Good of what is unfolding, dormant levels of intuition, strength and clarity become available to us. These qualities, as well as higher-frequency phenomena, will be in place to assist us through the wonderful changes that we have come to Earth to experience and support. Once we acknowledge them, miracles will become a part of our daily lives.

BE KIND TO YOURSELF

During these changes it is important to be kind to yourself. Rest, eat well, live in serene environments, trust your intuition and associate with like-minded people. There is nothing in our history that equals the magnitude of the changes occurring in our bodies now, so be kind to them.

Also be assured that as we raise our frequencies, we enter refined states of awareness where we see, feel and know more than we do now. Quickly we reach a place where our new world becomes a great adventure to experience and enjoy. Then we enter realms that exist simultaneously with our own. We can choose to be among many possible realities…including our present three-dimensional one. We are not leaving anything behind to go somewhere else. It is *all* available to us.

By vibrating at higher frequencies we become Light enough to change our form or shape. We can experience "Exchangeability," a process taught to me by *Exx*, my favorite dolphin, during our long swims together.

As we swam side by side in a state of deep peacefulness, *Exx* and I would exchange feelings, thoughts and bodies with each other.

People can learn to do this with other Beings also, as a way to get to know them and explore their different expressions of loving energy.

We can become *invisible,* travel through air, go places and then return to our third-dimensional, dense bodies. We can contact other entities, bathe ourselves in realms of Pure Light, enter group mind at will, communicate with universal information-systems, bi-locate, create specific energy fields for healing, purify environments and balance frequencies on small and large scales. The goal is to optimize ourselves (our cells) and the way we relate to the world around us. When we resonate together using the power of group mind as demonstrated by the dolphin pods, we construct a new planetary collective consciousness of compassion and peace. All of the Earth will benefit from our elevated awareness.

A NEW UNDERSTANDING OF HISTORY:
DOLPHINS COME THROUGH A WINDOW IN TIME

The dolphins taught me that things are not really as they seem, and encouraged me to stretch my mind to open to new possibilities in the reality of our world.

People are taught that dolphins have lived on this planet for millions of years, that they are highly evolved forms of life who maintain their societies on this planet without killing each other or damaging their environment. There are ancient Roman, Greek, Chinese and even Egyptian stories and myths about dolphins that indicate they have been rescuing and inspiring people for many ages. There are murals, frescoes, cave paintings and sculptures of them that date back thousands of years. I have often heard people say that they have "always loved dolphins," for as long as they can remember, and "since childhood." Hearing this, the monitor in my consciousness that discerns a hidden Truth from a popular belief goes off like a bell. I have sensed there is something about their feelings of connectedness to the dolphins that relates to an awareness beyond this lifetime, perhaps a parallel reality. The people expressing their love for the dolphins are sincere — I am sure of that — but I felt the intense feelings they experienced were another, as yet undisclosed, piece of the dolphin connection puzzle.

Why did my inner voice question the dolphins historical presence on this planet? In my curiosity, I delved into the history of Hawaii where the ancient people lived close to the sea. The Polynesians are known to be an 8,000 year old culture living in the middle of the Pacific Ocean, yet there is no mention of dolphins in their traditional chants and hula. When I asked my Hawaiian friend, a Kahuna of Chant, Hula and Laying on of Hands, why the dolphins were not mentioned, he very simply said, "They were not here."

When I turned to the dolphins to inquire about this, I was shown an amazing concept that opened my mind to reinterpreting my present reality. There are many occurrences in our lives of which we are unaware. I began to understand that life on Earth is different than what we may think.

The dolphins showed me an acoustic image of their arrival on the Earth plane. They arrived here through what they called "a window in time." But, it was not millions of years ago — it was during this century! At first I did not understand. They showed me how certain sound waves affect human activity on Earth, allowing spiritual beings to interact with the Earth's frequencies and bring in new sound-wave patterns that are beneficial and non intrusive. I was reminded of my experience of people "frozen in time" at *Oceansong* bookstore in 1978.

That event had eventually triggered a memory in me of advanced technologies with sound that exist among our galactic relatives.

During a high-frequency transmission from the *Spiritual Alliance*, the dolphins "arrived" on Earth, complete with all of their cetacean "history" on the planet. The Greek and Roman myths, the multi-cultural legends, stone carvings, cave art, artifacts, hieroglyphics, and so on, were all placed into the mind of humanity, into the many, varied locations on the planet and into our history books and archives. The reality of dolphins, from the past to the present, intellectually and physically, entered our mental and cellular awareness in a single instant. As far as humans are concerned the dolphins have always been here. But in Universal reality they are fairly recent residents of our globe! This instantaneous arrival on Earth was a galactic decision based on necessity. The *Spiritual Alliance* is a council of expanding fields of Light comprised of the most loving vibrating souls in our Universe. They have greatly advanced levels of consciousness in many worlds, serving both physical and nonphysical domains. As the guiding sentinels of our cosmos, they look forward to residents of Earth participating more fully in their multi-planetary overlighting of the community of souls, stars and planets in our galaxy. (*"Spiritual Alliance"* is not necessarily their name. Organizations of energy-beings are identified by their vibration, and so titles are not used. But since humans use names to identify and label fields of energy, the spiritual entities accommodate us by giving us a name to use. The *Spiritual Alliance* could just as easily be called *Celestial Hierarchy, Galactic Federation of Worlds* or the *Sisterhoods-Brotherhoods of Light*.)

The dolphins further explained, *"Because Earth people remain so immersed in physical reality and the belief systems that accompany physicality, it was determined that a physical expression could best be used as a way to open humans to their potentials as multi-dimensional beings."* To achieve this, a loving sea-being, the dolphin, was designated as the emissary to assist us in our evolution by taking a three-dimensional, physical form on Earth while teaching humankind about nonphysical realities.

The new dolphin and whale consciousness burst forth all around the world. In the United States the dolphins first spoke through the scientist, Dr. John Lilly, through the television program Flipper, and through the visionary artist, Jean-Luc Bozzoli — raising our awareness of their intelligent presence in the oceans and drawing attention to the life-sustaining necessities of the oxygen-producing ecosystems there.

One of their roles is to call attention to the oceans which are being polluted with toxins and Extra Low Frequency (ELF) waves. Some cetaceans make contact with human psyches by entangling themselves in fishing nets and dying on beaches, which forces people to examine the water and discover the problems. Hoping to make contact with as many Earthlings as possible, other dolphins encourage people to enter the water and swim with them.

The term "walk-ins" has become part of our vocabulary, as we meet more and more souls who have arrived on Earth in the physical in a way similar to the dolphins — to be rainbows of Light and conduits for cosmic beams of high-frequency energy. The dolphins are "swim-ins," entering the oceans and gaining our respect with their playful overtures of joy and freedom.

So what is the dolphins' plan? To enlighten the planet with their joy and beauty, their grace and love. To raise human consciousness about our oceans. To help people overcome a fear of deep water (and deep consciousness), by inviting us into their blue world. To trigger cellular memories of our universal connections. To remind us how to use vibrational frequencies to expand our minds into multiple realities. And to prepare people on Earth for the next millennium.

OPENING TO MULTIPLE REALITIES

Most of us are aware of only a small part of our world. The reality we accept is a minute layer of all that truly exists. Within this minute layer of existence we separate the physical world from the spirit world. Our beliefs do not acknowledge that these worlds cross back and forth into each other often.

This merging of different dimensions, of differing planes of existence, is occurring now, spontaneously, in our daily lives. Some people are aware of it, others are not. When we choose to prepare ourselves mentally, physically, emotionally and spiritually to cross thresholds of consciousness, our belief systems will expand to accommodate these unknown realms. When we swim with the dolphins, they transmit cellular codes to us that assist in our transformation and add the comfort of familiarity to our passage between worlds. Accept Everything! As we meet our true selves, learn to control our environment, and realize ourselves as cosmic citizens, we see a glimpse of the magnitude of our multi-dimensional reality. The Earth is becoming a fourth-dimensional star as part of her evolutionary process. And all of us residing on Earth are facilitating the shift of terrestrial consciousness.

What will this shift look like to us? Everything that is not of the Earth, that is not a natural earthly element, will disappear. Only soil, clay, wood, stone, water and biological matter will remain in our new reality. All man-made artificial and synthetic materials will be gone. There will be nothing in our world that is not vibrating at a fourth or fifth-dimensional level. When we look into the solar system, the constellations will have changed into a new skyscape of fourth and fifth-vibrational planets.

As fourth-dimensional beings we will also be able to dematerialize and levitate. Our bodies will take on new forms as all of matter around us changes. Solid objects in the next dimension have a different molecular structure. Fourth-dimensional beings can move through walls. For a while third and fourth-dimensional people will remain on Earth together. Subatomic particles move at different frequencies, and so even when occupying the same space, they do not collide with each other. Their frequencies put them in differing vibrational fields, preventing them from interacting. They can remain in the same space until the people who prefer to remain in third-dimensional reality pass on and reincarnate on another planet of duality. Eventually, only fourth-dimensional beings and higher, who are here to be *of Service*, will exist on the New Earth.

In the third dimension, people spend their lives sorting through emotional and intellectual issues and problems. This is the appropriate spiritual process for that level of evolution. In the fourth dimension, many more levels of inspiring information and vistas are available that utilize our untapped skills and potentials for accomplishing a new level of advanced spiritual work. An exciting and expansive world of universal potentials and adventures awaits us. By experiencing the shift, we open our minds to the vastness of the Universe and the multiple spiritual worlds that exist there. We welcome this opportunity to enter elevated frequencies of greater freedom, movement and thought.

Many high-frequency walk-ins are arriving now to be here during the transformation and to populate the new earth. At present, approximately one quarter of Earth's population is spiritually aware of their purposes and understand they are here to help people and the planet. Most of the rest of the people are still undecided.

As this highly refined energy approaches, our space brothers and sisters will assist us, especially our relatives from Sirius and the Pleiades. Their arrival is not determined by measurable movements of the planets and the motions of the galaxies, it is determined by the evolution of the spiritual beings on Earth. *We are calling for them.* We have reached a level of evolution whereby a higher consciousness flows through us and is becoming part of our molecular structure. It exists everywhere in the Universe and is vast beyond our imagination. Our interplanetary friends have access to this consciousness, and they are already merging with us on other levels. This consciousness moves into many dimensions, takes on many forms, divides and networks. It grows. It is not afraid of change. Why are we? Some ETs cannot understand why humans are so resistant to change.

The changes are accelerating, and for some people, releasing their familiar life scripts will be difficult. But in the cellular structure of our bodies we have memories from the very beginning of time that are responding to the intelligence in the Universal pool of knowledge. At the biological and soul level we already know we are here to evolve in service, and to change our forms as part of the process.

So often the teachings of the dolphins in the ocean, mirror galactic concepts. In the chapter about Participatory Research I described my interactions with a dolphin:

"When a dolphin swims towards me, I move into a parallel position alongside her and join her as any other dolphin would. I open myself empathically to the feelings and thoughts I receive in her presence. But I do not just passively record these, I also respond back to her, understanding that my response to her is as significant as her original communication to me. The research is about the interaction we share with each other. To accomplish this, it is important that I remain open to the unexpected, treat each exchange as unique, and resist any inclination to apply previously made interpretations to the interactions."

Reread this paragraph now, replacing "dolphin" with the words "Light Beings." The teachings about pod mind and pod families also relate to the New Earth, where learning to live in community with each other and practicing openhearted Love and Trust will be essential expressions of our spiritual selves.

After the fourth dimension and into the fifth dimension we will explore far reaches of the Universe and be able to communicate with beings of many vibrational frequencies. As we come to understand the structure of the Universe, we will become aware of the force of all Light and Love and learn how to construct universes of our own, based on compatibility with the greater cosmic plan of the Source.

In the fifth dimension we do not understand the purpose of evolution as education, but as service to the Divine Source. Doing exactly what the Divine Source would have us do in every moment. It is not about "healing the Earth" or "teaching humanity," it is a sharing of our Being for no reason. We have the urge to do something and we do it. We have the urge to say something and we say it. Every action and word that emerges from us is contributing to the system that co-creates the universe. It is a different consciousness. And if it seems to you that this appears threatening because it is so different, just remember that this Spirit, this Divine Source, is an expanded version of yourself and all you have done is to expand your identity. And in this expansion you have not given up anything. You do not lose your humanity, you include third and fourth-dimensional realities in your expansion into the fifth dimension. The greatness and fullness of who you are begins to be actualized in your body, mind and heart.

The Loving Energies of Your ET Sisters and Brothers

10

OUR COSMIC NEIGHBORS

And who are these ETs that we will meet and merge with? Are they us in the future? Are they Beings of Light? And how will we know that they are?

The extraterrestrials are beings who reside beyond Earth's belief systems. They are living in places that we cannot see, such as along the warm waterways of inner Earth accessible through the north pole, in subterranean dwellings, or under the sea. They are on other planets, in other time zones, and in places and realities unknown to us. Like us, they are an integral part of the universal plan for growth and evolution in our galaxy. They have different forms, organs and brains than we do. Some do not have the bicameral brain of the human race. They process information and emotions differently than us. The ETs who I meet have evolved beyond the earthly experiences of duality, of good and bad, black and white. They are on a path of evolution into the Light. Because they know what is good for one is good for All, they can live easily with group mind as the dolphins do. They have no hidden agendas, no individual self-seeking motives. They are aware of the Divine spiritual plan and they understand their role as expediters of the evolutionary expansion of Love and Peace in our solar system. As entities who are sustained by the Light, they have a complete understanding of our dual lives as physical beings and as soul beings on a very dense planet. They do not keep secrets or hide themselves from us. They are honest and answer our inquiries openly.

They experience our feelings and thoughts, and reflect them back to us. Nothing is concealed in their presence. They communicate equally with many cultures and people of all economic strata. In their truth, they reflect back to us our limited beliefs, and therefore many secrets hidden in thought patterns of humans, regarding fear, deception and greed are brought to Light.

We will know who they are because we have been preparing for many years to trust the intuition of our hearts. We are Beings of Light and Love and as we radiate that Truth, there is nothing to fear. When we eliminate fear (or lack of Love), the resonance of our hearts aligns us with kindred souls. Being in a feeling of Love, we attract only loving entities to us. Our reasoning minds can fool us, our hearts cannot. As we make contact with other loving races, also created in the image of God, we will resonate compatibly with them and the love in our hearts will give us the answers to our questions. We will know these people and remember our history with them in the cosmos.

It is important to understand the ETs' interactions with us. Our belief systems shape our reality. The ETs cannot approach us with Universal Love when our fears and misconceptions color our perception of them. They are waiting for us to become more aware of who we are, more at peace with their presence in our world, to open our understanding and our hearts to the ET civilizations who are our neighbors.

Because the time of great changes is approaching, the ETs have succeeded in making contact with us in a "grass roots," one-on-one mode. They would like the revelation of their existence to be announced by our world governments, who could host and support the communication between our races by explaining the ETs' humanitarian purposes in traveling to planet Earth. But because decades of their contacts with government and military personnel have been officially denied by the United States (and at the same time, labeled "Classified Information") our visitor friends have resorted to contacting individuals directly. They are helping us to recognize our Soul paths and understand that we are much more than our physical bodies. I am so grateful that they have persevered in meeting with us, in the light of all our fears and reservations. They are concerned for our well-being and the continuation of our civilization on planet Earth, and they are doing everything possible to enkindle our cosmic awareness, to nudge us in remembering the wonder of who we are.

Whitley Strieber, in his book *Breakthrough*, writes about his contacts with the ET visitors: "Many things have fallen away, many fears. For the visitors there remains only love, both for the part of them that appeals to me and the part that I find ugly...and all of the maddening, ambiguous things that fall between. In the same way that I have found real love for my fellow man and my own flawed self, I have found it for them. If we discovered a species at our own shuddering edge and had the capacity to literally pour ourselves into its life, we would make many mistakes. The visitors are as complicated as we are, and probably a lot more. In their overall approach to us in all of its ramifications, we are seeing the first true artifacts of their culture. A culture filled with differences just as ours is and also with a fear of us that must be at least as great as ours is of them."

Their fear of us appears to be "as great as ours is of them" because they often mirror our fearful perceptions and feelings. They communicate as a group with one mind and respond to the feelings and reactions of the people they meet. The entities from Sirius told me that Sirians are our "mirror," meaning that they reflect back to us our own behavior and attitudes. Sirius, the brightest star in the night sky, twenty times more luminous than the sun is known as Alpha Canis Majoris, the Dog Star. They are the dog star and half-seriously told me that we are the god star. Dog is god spelled backwards, a mirror image.

DOLPHINS PREPARE US

Like the dolphins, our ET friends are not here to teach us things we already know. They are asking us to move beyond our five senses, unplug from old behaviors and habits and utilize parts of our brains that have been dormant. They remain just beyond our ability to touch them physically so that we can learn to touch them and each other by expanding our minds. They will tempt us and intrigue us, they will playfully zoom in and out of our atmosphere, they will help us confront our limiting belief systems and reveal our potentials. The dolphins, behaving in the same way, have been serving as emissaries for the rest of the ETs. As we learn to appreciate the dolphins and their cheeky behavior with us, so can we learn to understand other cultures, different from our own, different in appearance and lifestyles, but nevertheless very much a part of our expanding reality on planet Earth.

MAKING CONTACT

There are many similarities between communicating with cetaceans and ETs. The dolphins are trying to make contact with us from oceans and rivers all around the world. They want to communicate with people, preferably in the ocean where we can experience their world of differing realities and vibrational frequencies. Here in Hawaii, where do I see the Spinner dolphins most frequently? Far out in the deep ocean? No, they are in the boat harbors, at the piers, near the hotels, the airport bays, the marine parks, the surfing beaches — all the public places frequented by people.

I feel this is also true with our outer-planetary friends who live on other worlds, in other spaces in Time. The ETs are trying however they can to meet us. As more and more of us feel willing to meet them, and open our beliefs to their existence, they will become visible to us.

WE DO NOT SEE THEM

People who are not familiar with the ocean often look at it and do not see the pods of dolphins and the whales swimming on the surface. It's surprising how often people cannot see them unless someone points them out. But when you spend time in the ocean, when you look at it for many hours, when you begin to notice its subtle movements and colorations, every nuance, then you become aware of all the life that exists close to its surface. This is similar to our unfamiliarity with NEVs — non-Earth vehicles. Most of us are unaware of the bodies of movement in our skies, such as clouds, comets, stars, planets, satellites and so on. On a daily basis, the average person rarely takes time to examine life in the sky. The ETs are there though...and a belief system that does not want to accept their existence will not see them.

THEY STAY JUST OUT OF REACH

In my years of swimming among the dolphin pods, I have learned not to touch them. In fact, they come much closer to swimmers who keep their hands at their sides. If people try to reach out and touch them, they will stay just out of reach. Their message for us is not about holding on and going for a ride. We already know how to do that and it teaches us very little. Instead they encourage us to learn about aspects of ourselves beyond our five senses. They want us to communicate with them in other ways.

And so do the ETs. Many people who search the skies for ETs wonder why they always seem to stay just "out of reach." In my own experience, the ETs are prepared to give us only as much knowledge as we need, to grow on our own. They are not here to force us to change. But they know that we have to change before we can go through the evolutionary transformation being offered to us. They are here to tempt us into taking new steps in opening our minds to alternate realities.

When dolphins sense people in the water are afraid of them, they keep at a distance. They do not want to cause *fear* in people. Similarly, our extraterrestrial relatives do not want to scare us. They would like us to overcome unnecessary fear. If they sense we are afraid they will approach us gingerly and casually. They will reflect our feelings.

DEVELOPING TRUST

When you come to know the Spinner dolphins and Humpback moms and babies, you trust them. You know they are gentle creatures who have different societal structures than ours, without war, aggression, competition, possessiveness, grudges, judgments or anger. The dolphins and whales are approachable and kind with each other and with us.

The ETs I know are the same way. They have no hidden agendas. They are interested in us and feel about us as we feel towards the dolphins…love, curiosity and protectiveness.

ATTITUDE CHANGES, HEALTH IMPROVES

After being with dolphins, people's lives change. Their lives have more meaning and direction. I have watched numerous seminar participants reevaluate their lives, return home to leave their jobs and start exciting, creative and fulfilling work. People feel healthier and happier, ready to face the world with a positive attitude.

After communicating with ETs, people's lives change. NASA astronauts such as Gordon Cooper, Edgar Mitchell, Brian O'Leary and Senator John Glenn who have traveled in outer space, inspire people with their messages of hope and truth. ET contactees become aware of their spiritual selves and choose new work in service to humanity, as revealed in the many case studies described in Dr. John Mack's book, *Abductions*. He calls the process an "evolution of consciousness." I have seen these life transitions in my counseling practice in Hawaii with clients who have been visited by ETs. In the United States there is an organized program involving counselors in every state who are willing to help people understand the magnitude of the changes that occur in their lives as a result of ET contacts, and prepare society for witnessing NEVs with ETs on board.

COMMUNICATING WITH POD MIND

Dolphins use more of their brains' capabilities than we do. The efficiency of their mode of communication becomes obvious in the wild, when they all move together as a unit, surf the waves at the same moment, make direction-changes simultaneously. Among adult Spinner dolphins, whatever one of the pod thinks and does, is good for everyone. When I swim among the dolphins I begin to read their group mind. I know where they are going before they get there. How can we develop instant, open communication like this? When will we live in a society like theirs? When we have no secrets, no hidden agendas, no negative reactions. This is achieved through truthfulness, integrity and Pod or Group Mind.

The ETs that I have met interact with each other through Group Mind. A successfully functioning Group Mind requires a civilization that is loving and thoughtful of each other, such as theirs is. What is good for one is good for all. When you "speak" to one, you speak to the entire race. That is why they usually refer to themselves as "We," rather than "I." They are all a reflection of each other, and that reflection is one of Love and Peace.

Meeting entities in other densities is the result of my years of swimming among dolphins and whales. The dolphins called me in 1975 and since 1984 I have been a student of the dolphin pods, becoming sensitive to their vibrations and sounds. As we swim together, we accelerate our mutual fields of energy and explore the invisible realms. Other spaces become visible to us as we travel into the fourth dimension and beyond.

TRAVELING INTO THE FUTURE

From the fourth dimension, I began traveling into the future. This was not difficult to do, since once I advanced beyond a certain vibrational stage, there were no time or place constraints. Time and space limitations are beliefs of third-dimensional Earth perceptions and do not exist once we go beyond Earth's atmosphere. Many people are aware of the concept of past life regression and of going back into their childhood. Experiencing this, people gain useful knowledge from viewing past-life existences that are overflowing into and affecting their current lives. It is intriguing to realize that in the same way we can regress into the past, we can also go forward and progress into our future lives. It is just a matter of shifting perceptions and awareness, like tuning in to a different radio station.

One day, I had the future of the Earth on my mind as I spiraled beyond my three-dimensional body. My thoughts brought me to the early 2000s. I knew I was not merely visualizing or imagining, I was actually in the future, in a vibrating energy-body slightly more refined than I have now. My reasoning mind had difficulty coming to terms with my belief systems. How could this be possible? How could I be visiting the future? For most of us this has not been possible previously. However because the tonal frequency of our home planet is accelerating, we can now do many things that were not possible before.

Looking around, I was amazed and then shocked. What I saw was traumatic — heat, winds, barren, dry earth, people surviving in rubble and caves, no water or food apparent anywhere. It was desolate. Although I had been teaching about Earth's geophysical changes, and was aware that they were pending, I was still unprepared for actually being there. For three weeks I ventured into this reality, observing and interacting with the survivors on the vast windswept plains of America. Often they were able to physically see me as I appeared in their caves and cabins, and talked with me about their lives. They were living in a new paradigm where telepathic communication was a skill used by most and the land continued to be the primary source for nourishment, although in many locations only underground plants could flourish. As the Earth completed her cleansing, I witnessed the arrival of huge spacecraft hovering and dispatching small ships to bring supplies and protein supplements to the residents of Earth. People were relocated to large space vehicle cities to wait for the atmosphere around the Earth to clear, to allow life to thrive again on Earth. People lived on these ships for four or more years protected from Earth's climate and erratic weather conditions. It became a temporary way of life for many who were here to assist after the earth changes and who were grateful for its shelter. Everyone had a role to play in this transformation of earth and her people. In the Earth's three-dimensional future, those who were long-term residents, returning for many incarnations, were encoded with the planet's matrix, which allowed them to remain on Earth during the geophysical changes. Those who were here as "walk-ins" from other star systems could not live on the earth during this transition, and so their frequencies were uplifted and they resided in other spaces until the Earth's energies were stabilized.

I went through a period of great sadness and resistance to these experiences, feeling deeply discouraged by the visual impact of the devastation on our once beautiful planet. I felt so much love for the Earth and was overwhelmed by the understanding that it was too late to reverse the changes. The point of no return had passed decades ago when we began experimenting with nuclear energy and other powerful frequencies without knowing the repercussions of their force fields in our atmosphere. Weather patterns had changed, the Earth was in transition. And many of us had known at a subconscious level that we incarnated here to be present during this epoch of change.

THERE IS MORE THAN ONE FUTURE

When I asked for guidance and love to help me be at peace with these revelations, I was advised to travel into the future again. I spent a few days in seclusion in my house preparing for my next journey. Then I once more entered deep meditation, experienced dolphin energies, chose a year and went there. I knew that strong emotions would cause me to waver out of alignment with the frequency-beyond-time and prevent me from staying there, so it was important to face the new world in which I found myself without fear or judgment. I began to enter other time-lines, looking over a wider area and observing the land. This was illuminating because now I saw other realities…communities in the mountains, areas with trees, green plants and fresh running water. There were people here, and they were living very well in these oases. This was more attractive, more positive, and I knew that it existed in tandem with the barren desert I had seen previously. I had shifted from a third-dimensional to fourth-dimensional plane. And suddenly I was filled with the knowledge that when I visited Earth's future in a fifth-dimensional frequency, I would see even more diverse views of reality.

We can visit our own futures and then come back and change them if we choose to. And as the dolphins have taught us, we can rewrite our past. In our world of time and space parameters, we understand our lives as occurring in a linear way in which we experience first our past, then our present and then our future. But from the dolphins' point of view, we actually transcend the time-space universe when we realize that our futures are already here and our present lives are simply another reality along a continuum of simultaneous events. Our life experiences are excerpts and incidences of life that are dotted all over the blank sheet of reality that is our personal map. We can pop into the All That Is at any time and place. If a line were drawn between the dots of our life-occurrences, it would not follow a straight line. The past, present and future are all in the here and now, occurring simultaneously. The past hasn't gone anywhere, we just can't see it. This is the reality in most of the universal worlds. We can learn to access that timeless space and choose where to visit in our own lives.

HOLDING THE VISION OF THE DOLPHINS

There is more than one future, and as I enjoyed my swims each day in the ocean with the dolphins, I wondered which one would be mine.

What is actually going to happen on Earth? There are many possible scenarios, and they all could manifest. However, what is important is that we know how to shift dimensions and are able to make conscious choices about where we want to be at any given time. Do we want to stay with three-dimensional material thoughtforms or do we want to interact with enlightened vibrations of Love from other planes of existence? Already many of my friends are choosing to withdraw their energies from the current thoughtforms on Earth. They refuse to view violent films or aggressive sports, or to have unfeeling friends or condone competitive thinking, or to support negative ideologies. They are choosing to create a gentle, loving world. They are increasing the love in their hearts while eliminating the discontent, anger and boredom from their lives. They have learned the importance of being happy.

As the significance of these time-traveling excursions becomes clear, I realize how wonderful it is to be able to travel into the future, see what is there, come back to a familiar reality here, and reevaluate my life in relation to what is ahead. Realizing I have a choice about what my future is, I spend many hours soul-searching. Am I to be among the dwellers of the barren deserts and contribute to rebuilding the Earth by assisting in the evolution of humanity's spirit, developing the intellect and psyche, experiencing unprecedented physical competence and endurance? Am I to live for years on an orbiting space vehicle and enter many realities to assist humanity energetically and spiritually? Am I to experience climatic changes in the mountains and live in a new, cooperative civilization focused on fulfilling our spiritual purposes and utilizing our inherent gifts? Or is my work on Earth completed, taking me to another planet beyond Earth? Our ET friends are demonstrating to us that we can do all of these things. When we recognize our capabilities as cosmic, spiritual beings and open our awareness to expanding our consciousness, we are no longer restricted to one location and one form.

One afternoon while I was in my living room receiving a Lomilomi massage, I bi-located into my bedroom where I was straightening the books and papers and putting away the laundry. Leaving my room to walk downstairs, I remembered that I was scheduled to have a massage and with that thought, I popped back into my body. I had been in physical form upstairs and I had continued to receive the massage downstairs at the same time. This kind of occurrence can happen more and more now as we open ourselves to multiple realities. Interestingly, I received confirmation of these things by two different friends from Florida and New York. One person experienced being underwater swimming with dolphins while walking along a street in San Diego. The other friend, while sitting on his front porch, bi-located to a residence a half mile from his home and rescued a toddler who had fallen unobserved into a backyard pool. The family was very grateful and the newspapers carried the story. Meanwhile he was trying to understand how he had rescued the child without ever having left his porch. These types of happenings raise many questions that shift our beliefs and accelerate our spiritual growth. They are becoming more common as we accept our inherent ability to immerse ourselves into simultaneous, multiple worlds.

We have a choice to remain closed, or to open to multiple realities. All the questions we have assist us in delving more deeply into our self- education. People often tell me about an unusual experience they have had with the dolphins, whales or ETs, and they ask what it means. What is the truth of the experience, is it positive or negative, real or a dream? Are the entities loving or dangerous? How does it relate to their present lives? Is it an omen? A message? How should it be interpreted? In the rational world, our security lies in clear answers to these questions. But I have learned that the journey into enlightenment is not about the right answers, it is about following the complexity of the questioning mind into more and more self-education. In our search to find answers to our questions we attend workshops, read books, meet new people, go to distant places, open ourselves to new realities and prepare ourselves for entering our futures. If all of our questions were answered, we would cease to grow. The more we question, the more we open to possible answers. Suddenly the importance of our lives on Earth and the preciousness of every moment becomes apparent to us. What is more important than preparing ourselves for our futures? For being living examples of our futures now? We are spiritual beings incarnated on Earth at this time for a reason. Our time has come and our real work is beginning — the work of assisting our Earth through the unfolding Transformation.

As we evolve into cosmic beings, readily accessing many realms of Light and Love, we are in contact with the Angelic Beings who are guiding us. For many years we have asked for clarity about our roles in the Universe and now we are seeing them clearly. There is a wonderful world opening to us — a place of Joy and Inspiration and Peace. This is what the dolphins are teaching us…to be able to accept their lifestyle, their world of happiness and fulfillment. In the days ahead we will live more like dolphins and we will play among many worlds. So keep the vision of the dolphins in your minds and hearts. As we seek the highest guidance and ask for direction and healing, our questions find answers and new masteries of our subtle and physical bodies are learned. These new abilities and understandings will make the times of change easy and joyful for us. The new worlds we will enter, the new visions we will see, the new bodies and minds we will express in our multiple expanded dimensions will thrill and fulfill us beyond our present imagination. I have seen the spiritual path of humanity and it is one of highly developed creativity, sensitivity and enlightenment. I am filled with so much gratitude and anticipation for the beauty of our new and expanded world. It will infuse us with meaning, productivity and self-realization. The world will be a place where fulfilling spiritual goals is the essence of community life and everyone does what they enjoy as a productive and independent member of society, a family of Light.

11

YOU
ARE THE LIGHT

I continued to swim with the dolphins regularly, enjoying peaceful, states of pod mind with them. I experienced the dolphins most purely when I could maintain a balanced, stress-free environment at home in my daily life. But as more and more people were called by the dolphins to come and swim, the schedule of my Ocean Seminars grew so full I had little time to explore these altered states of consciousness. And so in 1994, I decided to give the leadership of Dolphin Swim Programs to my dear friends and co-workers, Trish Regan and Doug Hackett. I knew they would carry on the work with the love and attention it deserved.

ALTERNATE REALITIES

Now I had more alone time to spend in interdimensional frequencies with the dolphins and whales. Soon I began to easily enter alternate realities while in deep meditation. The dolphins and whales were introducing me to the next step in my evolutionary development. I was being shown how to access the world of my Soul, a world where I learned that I am a multi-dimensional being who is much more than a third-dimensional, physical body.

As I continued to meditate and travel into other realities, I understood its usefulness in expanding my unlimited mind. How wonderful to be able to shift frequencies into other realms whenever I wanted to visit someone, view other geographical locations, gather information, change my vibrations, understand past memories or enter the future. The uses were extensive. We live in a much larger world than I was aware of for most of my Earth life…and now I was ready to explore it.

TRAVELING TO OTHER REALMS

Since I was traveling in unknown places, I repeatedly asked my guides to surround me with the Light of Love as I continued my quest for more knowledge. They obviously were assisting me along my new path. One day in August, 1996 I dreamed that I met a gentle Light Being who identified himself as Robert Monroe, a previously incarnated pioneer in the consciousness movement. This being, appearing very human in a shirt and slacks, encouraged me to contact the Monroe Institute in Faber, Virginia. I remembered that Monroe had an interest in dolphins because in 1994 someone phoned me on his behalf to inquire about my dolphin communication programs. Subsequently I learned that the Institute had a Dolphin Energy Club for healing people through pod-mind energy. In the same way that the dolphins synchronized the hemispheres of my brain using their sounds and sonar, Monroe had developed brain hemispheric synchronization tapes to produce sound patterns to stimulate whole-brain functioning. This learning tool helps people gain control of their awareness-expansion and communicate with other energy beings and realities. I called the Institute immediately and reserved a space in their program. My goal was to learn a more disciplined method of traveling to other realms to complement my spontaneous experiences and to learn about my soul's potentials through Monroe's teachings.

Participating in the programs of the Monroe Institute, I used hemispheric synchronization music and guided meditations to enter and exit other realms with speed and precision.

ASPECTS OF MY SOUL

When I first ventured into these realms, I met with a group of Light Beings whose countenance filled me with great love and peace. I recognized them as Beings I had known all my life. In spiritual realms we would sit, dressed alike in white robes in a circle on a grassy knoll in the shade of trees and enthusiastically share our recent excursions to different planets, in different realities. The hills were populated with many groups sitting comfortably in circles. Souls were coming and going from groups numbering twelve or thirteen. Our thoughts were so harmonious they created a sound like music. I noticed the presence of animals around us, horses, cows, cats, gentle dogs, birds, little animals who were nearby and could communicate with us. There was a familiarity to this place. I knew I had been here before and had sat as one of the white-robed beings who were my friends. It was so inspiring to share our stories of multiple dimensions, physical experiences, feelings of merging with the oneness of Realms of Light, as we enjoyed our reunion. With this contact I understood the Truth as revealed by Jesus and other Ascended Masters when they said we never die. Physical bodies drop away, but the spirit, the soul and our personalities, all spiritual knowledge and memories, feelings, remain with us. We are the same person we are now as we enter other dimensions and go on to our next exciting adventure.

As I continued to visit this spiritual state, given the name of "Focus 27" by Monroe, I referred to these Light Beings as my guides. Whenever I left Focus 27 to visit other dimensions these Beings would accompany me. Eventually I came to know them as eleven aspects of my soul who were living in realities parallel to my own, some incarnated on earth, some incarnated on other planets and some remaining in the etheric realms. I could travel with them to "their" realities and view the alternate parts of myself that were creating different group units, different experiences, and different light-waves.

SOUL TRAVEL

I have had fascinating contacts with other aspects of my soul cluster. By following a band of directed Light, I found one aspect of my soul is a baby in India. I have traveled this baby's energy line to see her future path. This child will be going through the Earth changes on planet Earth. She has reached the Earth plane with an evolved frequency of Light that will transmute her into the fourth dimension as needed. In addition she does not have the belief system that says she has to eat food to survive. She will know how to survive without food and will be able to live on energy. And she is the aspect of myself who will go through the earth changes in the physical so that I can benefit from it, gaining information from the Earth in transition and coming in and out through her soul-being whenever I want to.

I have traveled the bands of energy to another part of my soul which has been living in a colorful energy field among the particles of space, enjoying many, many years of being in complete bliss and fulfillment...a part of the oneness of all.

Another aspect of myself is incarnated among a civilization of extraterrestrials who have learned to access multiple dimensions easily in their everyday lives. They can shift frequencies readily. This is probably why I am so interested in this subject in my present incarnation. The aspect of my soul that is part of their civilization can go through solid objects, dematerialize and rematerialize and travel easily around the universe. There, I am part of a society at peace with itself. No aspects of myself need to deal with war and violence anymore. The twelve aspects of my soul have evolved beyond that level of emotionalism and physical challenge. This is certainly why I cannot relate to the games of war being acted out on Earth in this physical experience. That is no longer part of my reality. I am enjoying contacting and learning from the different soul aspects of myself.

Making this soul contact has helped me understand how universal our souls are and how much we know at our spiritual levels. We have a vast, untapped Creative energy called the Soul and we can shift our biological perspective and gain access to the wisdom of the Soul while we are still physically incarnated.

BEING IN SERVICE

One day I asked how I could use my ability to access multiple realities to be of Service in the spiritual realms. I was shown that in the event of "future" earth changes many souls would choose transition and, due to the huge ring of heavy frequencies around the earth (an energy field created from centuries of emotions and limiting beliefs,) it could be difficult for these souls to move on. I was shown an area where many soul-people were surrounded by a billowing gray cloud. I could not see them clearly because the grayness around them was thick and dark. When I inquired about their identities, I received that they were "lost souls," or people who had died but had not gone into the Light. The Light was there, but the people had not entered it. The Light looked like a tube of energy. It transported souls to high-frequency locations to meet their guides and then go on to their next evolutionary existence. The souls in the gray areas had not believed in life after death. Their belief systems said that once you die, there is nothing. And so they remained confined to this space, without direction or movement, until they could release their limiting beliefs and seek freedom.

As more and more souls enter this gray mass of unclarity around the earth plane, the density of the cloud will thicken and souls will be unable to extricate themselves. Spiritual beings in the higher realms are concerned about this, because the density is so thick around the earth it is difficult for master guides and disincarnate spiritual brothers and sisters to enter the earth's atmosphere to assist. Some individuals incarnated on earth are being asked to help by contacting these lost and trapped souls and escorting them to higher dimensions where they can continue their souls' journeys. People on earth are more adept at dealing with the extreme emotional frequencies that occur here. There will be more and more heightened emotional vibrations as earth is transformed geophysically. We can assist our spiritual guides and our fellow earthlings by contacting, communicating and when appropriate, releasing these confused souls.

I visited this energy field with my guides. Not sure what to do, I telepathically called out, "Does anyone want help?" At this, many hands protruded from the gray cloud and a murmur of silent voices asked for assistance. I reached to make contact and found I could easily grasp one of the hands, and gave a tug. The soul-person floated upward toward me and together, holding hands, we located a tube of Light to enter. As we moved through this field of energy, I talked with the soul and learned the details of its physical life and death on earth. I repeated this process with many souls. My intent was to accompany the souls to Focus 27 where they could meet with their departed relatives or spiritual guides. Often, however, we did not get far before the person, now free from the belief in darkness-after-death, chose to stop along the way and in so doing, disappeared from my side. Later I learned that these unexpected departures were due to the soul's desire to visit other belief systems in the etheric realms. Every belief that humans have created with their thoughts exists in the astral planes. Some souls find a reality that suits them and choose to remain there.

It is very inspiring to assist soul-beings into the higher rays of Light where they are at peace and enjoy themselves, aware once again of themselves as spiritual beings who never die but live on. It is uplifting to see the joy of the people as they realize this, and the joy of their relatives and friends as they gather together in the Light. I am filled with deep gratitude to my guides for taking me there.

MANIFESTED BELIEFS

Visiting the area of "belief systems" through the guidance of the Monroe Institute, I saw countless realities that exist in the beliefs of what people expect after death. Stretching as far as I could see, there were many scenes. Mile upon mile, I saw hundreds of thousands of manifested realities of the beliefs held by people on Earth. These included areas of angels with big fluttering wings receiving newcomers, and an elderly, white-haired bearded man (GOD) opening his arms to people. There was Jesus on the cross and a robed woman, maybe Saint Mary, welcoming people. I saw lines of religious men in tall pointed hats and long, flowing purple-black robes receiving people. I saw symbols of many known and unknown religions. Some people were going to an area where lions, lambs, rabbits and other animals lived peaceably together. I saw people/souls riding off on white steeds with manes and tails flying, I saw people being taken on horse-drawn chariots. I saw aboriginal people returning to their ancestors in the stars, being floated straight up into a star. I even saw Disneyland — looked like the Magic Castle. I saw a sainted man standing at the gate of a fenced-in area. He had a list and was checking off names as people approached. The gates were made of pearls, so I guess this was Saint Peter. The people he rejected went to a gray area where everyone was moaning, crying, depressed, asking for forgiveness. They were contained in a small area, a teeming mass of misery, having to repent. I saw many areas where people roamed in nature. These were the beautiful, heavenly kingdoms. Some people floated among cloud formations and sat blissfully on soft white clouds. There were beautiful architectural structures, churches and temples, that were created by the thoughtforms of people who recalled childhood teachings from the sacred texts of their religions and interpreted them in their own mind. Souls were residing in these realities based on their beliefs about life after death.

THE GATHERING PLACE

Next I traveled to a "Gathering Place" for souls called the "Reception Center" by Monroe, a place created for easing the shock of transition out of physical reality, for resting and being nurtured while evaluating the choices for the next incarnation of spiritual evolution. It is a beautiful place with trees and flowers, lawns and paths and park benches and Beings walking, sitting, talking with old friends and new ones, enjoying themselves. I wanted to talk to people and ask them why they were here, where they came from, where they were going, but before I could do so, I was surprised to see my maternal grandparents. As I greeted them warmly and shared a hug, I wondered if my father was there. With that thought I saw my dad walking briskly toward me down the path in his characteristic gait. Great waves of love flowed through me as I walked to meet him. Dad left the Earth plane ten years ago, but now he was walking toward me, happy to see me, holding out his arms. We embraced. He seemed surprised and pleased to see me there. We quickly sat down and talked animatedly with the same camaraderie we had experienced on the earth plane. Kindred souls reunited.

He described his current work in this realm and I asked him if I could go with him to see his new location and his new occupation. He studied me briefly, as if to check my vibrational tenacity and then agreed. We floated upward together hand in hand, very expansive, moving out, out, out, into ever widening currents of Light that curved away from us, to a place where he is part of a soul-group creating a new planet. Interestingly, they have recreated the planet known as Earth — feeling that it was important to have a duplicate of it, to redo the human experience of incarnations on a planet of duality. Different time zones are indistinguishable here, and this planet is the Earth of the future, a beautiful place. It is created without any of the problems, toxins or pollution that plague the present Earth. I was deeply touched by its beauty and the purity and sweet fragrance of the air. Everything grows in lush abundance, the oceans and rivers are sparkling clean. Soon this planet will be completed and ready to host human civilization. After watching the soul-beings moving around the new Earth, sending showers of healing, restorative energy and sculpting it, we returned to the Gathering Place. I was prepared to sit and enjoy hearing more about Dad's adventures, when my Earthly physical body experienced a distraction that signaled I must return. We parted joyfully, knowing we could reconnect easily from now on.

HALL OF CHOICES

The next day I was drawn to another part of the Gathering Place. This is a huge area where people go to decide what their next span of existence will be, whether they want to incarnate in a physical body, an etheric body or remain as an energy particle for a millennium. It's a fascinating place that I call the Hall of Choices. Every type of soul expression is available along the continuum of an individual's evolutionary path. These soul choices correlate with different planets, different geometry, spirals and places in the universe that are working on that particular soul objective. As I observed, I saw people choosing incarnations to enhance their spiritual growth. They were continuing to study whatever was of interest to them, or whatever parts of their psyches they were working on in their parallel realities. There were energy stations and planets for every experience a soul might like. There were places where people could go to learn how to ascend while in the physical body, and other places where people could go to reconnect with their soul groups to work through emotional and intellectual issues. There were places to work through the different feelings that are represented as vibrations, to experience a full spectrum of realities. There were places people could go to experience being pure energy without physical form, taking time to enhance their vibrations. Some people who had left their previous lives with unresolved fears, such as fear of death, fear of abandonment, fear of separation from the Source, came here to choose lives where they could learn to overcome their fears.

In the Gathering Place, people locate areas in the galaxy and beyond which host the teachings to overcome these fears and then choose their next incarnation accordingly. Often they are correlating their new choices with the life experiences of the other aspects of themselves. Although other aspects of our souls are in different experiences and time zones, and may not have completed their physical lives as yet, they come to this location from their existences during sleep states, where together they all communicate and see how they can compatibly serve each other and the entity who is moving through the Gathering Center to choose its new life. It's all very cooperative. There is compassionate interest and assistance amongst the soul aspects. There are many ideas. It's an exciting place, filled with possibilities. Through a communication which telepathically and visually reviews experiences people have already had, it soon becomes quite clear what their next step could be. There is an accumulation of experiences that needs to be fulfilled before a soul can go on to the next level. Some aspects of a soul may still be in one level, while other aspects may be moving ahead, but they are all in contact with each other. It's a wonderful opportunity to learn and grow.

GROUP THOUGHTFORMS

During my soul journeys, I enter the future and assist souls at events that are occurring there. During these experiences, I visit parts of the United States and the Pacific Ocean to see their future realities. These realities are based on a confluence of present vibrational frequencies or thoughts emanating from Earth. Since group mind and the attraction between compatible energies influence earth's manifestations, it is easy to determine what the future holds for the human race. There are many negative thoughts and actions currently creating frequencies which are changing the form of the earth. This is the result of years of unconscious behavior and emotions which have set into place certain energy upwellings.

I have been shown that some realities will change and some will not change due to the continuation of old thoughtforms and actions which are affecting the Earth. When thoughtfully manifesting our own personal realities, we can write the script ourselves. But when the reality is global, and based on the thoughtforms of a group of earth beings, the outcome can be changed only if enough people join together and shift the thoughts of the collective consciousness of the whole earth. If that cooperative action does not happen, we can still choose our personal future in relation to mass reality. This is why it is important to visit the future, look at the options and create our personal reality with awareness, integrity and ingenuity. In the realms beyond our personal psyche, we can join with other spiritual entities to become part of a pod mind.

We can create positive futures for ourselves. When experiencing soul travel or sojourns into the future, I am aware of being two places at once. I am in another refined reality while I am also aware of my physical, three-dimensional self in my temporal reality. My brain and my body can have awarenesses separate from each other. This is a process the dolphins use frequently.

Interestingly, researchers in morphogenetic development say human genes do not contain enough information on their own to convert a cluster of cells into an embryo or to create a new life form. However a morphogenetic field effect (group mind) can be used to switch on specific genes and turn off other genes. The information in the morphogenetic field-pool contains much more data than an individual gene pool, and can be used to control gene expression (Cohen, Philip, "Child's lethal gene fault heals itself," *New Scientist*, July 20, 1996). People who do soul traveling evolve their morphogenetic fields from primary consciousness to high energy conscious-ness as they merge with other soul-beings and access the potentials of group co-creation.

I began spending more time traveling with my guides, to meet with higher aspects of my soul to review experiences from my Earthly past that were affecting the clarity of my soul's Light and the stability of my frequency. The veil between different realities became more transparent. Sometimes the new dimensions I explored would come to the surface while I was swimming or driving or even having a conversation with someone.

SOUL TRAVEL JOURNAL
The Soul of a Baby

Today, while meeting with a group of people, I suddenly become aware of the soul of a baby attempting to make contact with me. The infant's eyes are really bright, lovingly entering my consciousness. The feelings from it are so strong that I am overwhelmed with emo-tions. I quickly complete my meeting, so I can go into a quiet meditation and learn what this little soul wants.

Now I am alone and I contact the soul of that little child with the sparkling eyes that are so captivating. She communicates to me that we met in Florida when I was a Child Protective Counselor with the State Police. Together we spiral back in time to 1980 when I received an emer-gency call from Florida Health Services about a baby who needed help. I relive going to her home, see her lying inert in her crib, dying of starvation. What a shock to see her tiny form, much smaller than her age of nine months. There is hardly anything left of her body, just a skeleton. Little fingers that are mere bones, toes that are stumps, fleshless legs. My eyes make contact with hers. They are bright, filled with the perceptive wisdom of her soul. Instinctively I pick her up and hold her. Her soul reaches out, her tiny fingers clutch my dress, clinging in despera-tion. Without hesitation, I bring her to the hospital to try to save her life.

Now that little soul is here, taking me to connect with the souls of other babies that I knew in my work as a Counselor, babies who died. I reexperience the sadness, finding the children in pain, rescuing them and taking them to the hospital, being their voice in court and counseling their parents, turning them over to some other agency for long-term care. I don't see them again. Months pass, and I learn that they have been returned to their abusive families and have been killed or have died, and I am left with grief. Unexpressed grief that saddens my heart.

The little soul travels into the past with me to California, to meet the souls of some babies that are being aborted in a clinic where I am the psychologist. My job is to hold the hands of the distraught mothers and comfort them in the operating room. Now I see the souls of those babies, next to me, thanking me for being here, for helping them through their transitions. They felt my love and compassion and they are telling me that it helped them to go into the Light. I am aware of them leaving the body of the mother and leaving their own body. They communicate with me and make me aware of the complexity of abortion issues. They have chosen their parents and the circumstances of this incarnation with awareness and wisdom. They understand it served a purpose. Some parents are learning the lesson of compassion, about making decisions, about the powerful, debilitating effect of society's belief systems on their psyches. Some babies intentionally come in for only a few weeks in cooperation with the parents to complete their cycle of incarnations on the earth plane. Some babies choose abortion to assist in reviving the spiritual issue of life and death on earth, to remind people of the value of human life, to help people analyze and question their belief systems. There are many different reasons why these babies are aborting. They tell me that my love helps them make the transition meaningful and gentle, and that they have come from all the different worlds where they now live to resume the form of tiny souls to thank me. I feel their happiness being transmitted to me. It is an expression of their appreciation and I am filled with joy and peace.

And now the little soul-being, the one that first contacted me, is joining me on a soul assistance mission in Biafra, Nigeria. As we easily float there, I see many babies that are starving, their stomachs distended. They are leaving their bodies, they are dying. And I am here to see the release of their souls into freedom. As the ephemeral soul-beings transcend their bodies, I experience the joy of the soul spirits as they leave the physical. They are perfectly well…healed, complete, light and happy. Regardless of what happens on the physical plane the soul remains free and well. And now the souls of the different babies communicate with me, tell me that they want me to witness this because they realize that in my physical reality I only see the earthbound side of their passing — the pain and the sadness. And I have held deep memories of that sadness in me. Now, because I have learned to make soul contact, they are relieving me of my pain and sadness, awakening me to their joy, so that I will know the beauty of death and won't hold the sadness in my body and in my heart any longer. And so I witness the souls of these tiny ones leaving their bodies, flying free with great joy and happiness. As I watch, the old pain in my heart dissolves and I am at peace, giving thanks to this bright-eyed soul for taking me on this journey. A journey where the experience of Love is the most direct route to open the heart and access higher dimensions.

I continue to make excursions into other planes of reality, escorting lost souls caught in the gray emptiness encircling the Earth to the Light of higher dimensions. In addition I have been shown the reality of unending life, so that I can help myself and others know that we survive physical death. We don't ever die. We go on and on, individually and in soul groups, continuing to expand, learn, travel and make choices. It is fascinating and of course very familiar because our higher self already knows this.

SOUL TRAVEL JOURNAL
Visiting 2005

Becoming very relaxed and moving easily into a vibrational frequency beyond time, I contact my guides…"I ask all of my spiritual guides, the many aspects of myself, my higher self, and the ascended masters to be with me and take me to places that I have not been before. Bring me to soul assistance work that is useful and beneficial to others. Bring me to places beyond the Universe that I haven't seen. Bring me to places of frequency and Light that will enhance my physical and subtle bodies. I ask that I be shown any other pieces of information that are helpful for my own evolution and the evolution of people on planet earth. I ask for Guidance. I have set aside fear and resistance and I am open to every uplifting experience. My heart is filled with gratitude for your love, for your direction. I am so happy to be One with you. Thank you." I now expand into Universal Oneness.

My guides are with me and I ask to go into the future. We promptly arrive at 2005, present Earth. We have returned to the original location I visited in August. Above the United States I travel from the West Coast in an easterly direction and come to the Rocky Mountains. Instantly I realize with a jolt to my heart that I have come to my "future" home. I am living here in 2005. And I understand that I am to now purchase land or to become involved in a Center in this location in Colorado, in the high desert, surrounded by mountains. Being there, I feel a very strong reaction to this place, an emotional recognition, to my eventual home. A group of us have created a place where people come to have food, rest, nurturing and inspiration. I am watching many people passing through this location which is a "rescue/assistance" center on the earth plane in the year 2005 and beyond.

Interestingly, the work we are doing there continues the teachings of the dolphins regarding communication. We are going into other dimensions. There, we make contact with aspects of the souls of other Earth people, communicating with them and learning what is happening around the world. It is part of our research to access the nonphysical aspects of ourselves as a means of sharing information worldwide in a fourth-dimensional communication network. We developed the ability to meet periodically at a soul level and keep each other informed of what was going on globally, helping each other develop food sources and alternative paradigms for healthy living. Life enhancing belief systems grew from experiencing our Oneness in the fourth and fifth dimensions on Earth.

EARTH COMMUNICATION CENTER ORGANIZATION

Upon returning I thought about how people on Earth would have intuitive, psychic means of communicating in the near future. Where could we all go to share our knowledge when we are transitioning into the fourth dimension and the Earth's communication systems are down? When the computers, phones, facsimiles, televisions, satellites are no longer operating? I returned to the Gathering Place to choose a location where loving souls would convene. Seeing all the gardens and temples created by visiting entities for their own places of inspiration and nurturance, I decided to do likewise and create a Center for our future communication network. It is easily visualized as a huge transparent dome that enhances the communication process by it's curved architecture. The ceiling glows with brilliant, white stars against a royal blue background. Everyone who visits the Gathering Place can locate this Center from a distance, it is easily identifiable. Keeping this vision in mind, Earth people can bi-locate and meet there whenever Earth changes occur, to seek information or to share some, to recuperate, reacclimate and reunite with our terrestrial and cosmic families. There we can share the resources and knowledge of small communities scattered in locations around the planet, exploring methods of instantaneous healing, soul assistance, cooperative projects, food and water resources, interplanetary travel, new technologies, galactic updates, research and inspiration. It is a wonderful link for all kindred souls to access at will. The transparent dome has been named ECCO or Earth Communication Center Organization. By thinking the code word ECCO, we immediately access its rarefied environment where telepathic messages are transmitted and received by every Light Being present. The focus is on humanitarian consultation and assistance for communities on Earth. I encourage people to practice visiting there now. Your higher self will receive the code word ECCO and take you there as soon as you open your heart to that experience. The Center is filled with Light Beings who are in service to the evolution of Light and Love in our Universe.

INTO THE FUTURE SEMINARS

My enjoyment in traveling to these wondrous and enlightening places led to a desire to soul travel with other people and to benefit from the power of pod mind as taught by the dolphins. Understanding the evolutionary mind-expansion of this process encouraged me to teach it to those who are interested and ready to open their loving hearts to these experiences. The dolphins and I are conducting Into The Future Seminars in Hawaii. Through the gentle love and tender guidance of the dolphins we enter worlds beyond fear and we are rewarded by communication with angelic Light Beings, loving souls and fascinating journeys with soul groups of our multifaceted selves.

As we look to create communities together on Earth, we are supported by our already existing soul connections in communities in the etheric realms. Together we move into higher fields of consciousness, where many other beings of Light reside and await our arrival, to show us magnificent worlds that exist just beyond our ability to see. Having evolved through channeling, dreaming and remote traveling, we now *physically* enter the worlds with these spiritual Beings and visit their many realms of life. They escort us and endow us with a Universal awareness of Earth's *future* and our role in it — stimulating our own wisdom of ourselves in these parallel and future realities.

After fourteen years of communicating and swimming with dolphins and whales, out of body experiences and altered states of consciousness in the warm ocean waters of Hawaii have become common place at Dolphin Connection. The dolphins are helping us change the vibrational frequency of our physical matter through tones, directed rays of Light and adjustments to our belief systems. As spiritual people we are already open to these experiences, only needing to be guided into the parallel realities and refined states of living that exist close to our hearts, around us. Surrounded by Beauty, we gently access the unknown realms of who we are in our subtle bodies and in relation to the other loving beings who share the cosmos with us, living in fourth dimensional realities to prepare our physical forms and our psyche for our *future* lives. The ambiance of Hawaii allows us to remain in this rarefied domain of fourth dimension. Using the teachings of our joyful dolphin friends, we examine the significance of our service to others during these times of Change. This is why we are here — to participate in this great expansion of humanity into higher states of consciousness.

UNITED STAR UNIVERSES

The dolphins and whales have done their jobs well as awakeners so that we can love ourselves and recognize our spiritual love as the sacred vibration of Oneness. It is important to meditate regularly to keep outer conditions from affecting us. In every way it is important to keep your emotions and thoughts harmonious. If the fullness of inner Love and Happiness is to be expressed by you, Peace and Serenity in your personal life is essential. The feelings of Love and Harmony cannot be stressed too strongly. It is only within these vibrations that the power of Love's Light, the power of unlimited reality, can be actualized. The continual outpouring of Peace and Divine Love to every person and everything unconditionally, no matter whether you think it is deserved or not, is the Spiritual Key that unlocks the door and releases large increments of inner power. Once you experience this way of thinking and feeling, then you become Peace and Love. Harmony in your daily life is the answer. With it, all that is good and desired can be manifested — without it, all form disintegrates and returns to the Universal pool.

As your Light and Love fills every moment, your life unfolds your spiritual purpose for you. There is nothing else you need do. Know that all that exists is of Love, and as you perceive it, so you are immersed in it. Then enjoy your life, laugh often, visit realms of Beauty and accept that this is your world — a world of Goodness.

Meet me at *ECCO* and always remember: You Are The Light. We are now co-creating a new world and traveling the United Star Universes together Into The Future.

April 17, 1990

Swimming in the deep blue ocean, far from land, all around me are Spotted dolphins, hundreds of them. Silver-streaked, white-spotted forms gliding by, curiously turning their heads, wrinkling their necks to look at me. I am in their midst, filled with contentment and happiness as they sonar me and fill me with their sounds. Wanting to communicate and return their exuberance, I start to make noises, while still swimming gently in the ocean, caressed by the warm water. Squealing, shrieking, laughing, sending out my high-pitched notes, I look into their eyes. My sounds are different from theirs. They use the tonal language of the Spotted dolphin pods but I am speaking as a Hawaiian Spinner dolphin. They accept the difference and shrill back with sounds that pierce the silent ocean and resonate in my body.

Continuing to make sounds, I suddenly hear a faint echo of my own voice. Along with the Spotted's whistles, I am vibrating with other sounds similar to my own. Scanning the water in all directions I gradually see a formation of dolphins approaching me directly, coming as a unit, threading their way through the Spotteds. Adjusting my underwater vision I stare in disbelief as I recognize my family — a pod of Hawaiian Spinners, here, so far from shore, out in the deep ocean, responding to my vocalizations. My heart sings with love as I recognize my close friends, the Spinners, swimming side by side with me and the Spotteds.

I become a dolphin. I am accepted and included as one of the pod. My sounds sliced through the water, perhaps the shrillness of my voice sent a message that I was a lost dolphin, separated from my pod, seeking my soul family and the communion we share. And this Spinner dolphin pod responded to my call. Quickly they realize I am not in danger and their rescue mission becomes an enjoyable swim among playful Light Beings, dolphin cousins and their funny human counterpart. In shimmering rays of white Light, we swim together, knowing unending love in our oneness with Peace and Beauty…

Joan Ocean, M.S.

The evolution of human beings through gentle enlightenment and natural joy has been the center of Joan Ocean's work for the past twenty seven years. With a Master of Science in Counseling Psychology, Ms. Ocean is a psychologist and scientist who creates environments that support people in transition from one life style and one physical form to another. In 1984, with Jean-Luc Bozzoli, she cofounded Dolphin Connection, an organization which explores the advancement of human potentials through visionary films, books, art and interactions with free-swimming dolphins and whales. Ms. Ocean is the originator of human-dolphin swim programs in the world's oceans and rivers, providing safe passage and deep communication between humans and dolphins using empathy, biophysical vibrations and holographic, acoustic imagery. By invitation, Ms. Ocean is a member of the family dolphin Pods A, B and C at her Dolphin Connection Center in Kona, Hawaii. She enthusiastically dedicates her days to studying dolphins and whales by respectfully joining them in their natural habitats and becoming their friend.

Joan, Suchi Psarakos, and John Float

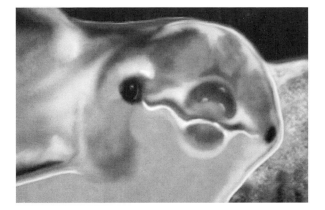

The cover of *Dolphins Into The Future* was designed and created by Jean-Luc Bozzoli, visionary artist. In addition, he contributed many of his art images and photographs to enhance the stories and inspired messages of the dolphins.

Jean-Luc Bozzoli's Artform whispers that we are more than we think, as he creates spaces of Beauty inspired by the geometries of organic and holographic pictographs from our vast, still to be explored natural world.

When we enter these fields, the colorful scenes activate deep feelings and memories of the many realms of our inner and outer universe.

Jean-Luc's art, shows and videos are available through:

Eye Within Studios

Telephone and Fax: 1-800-555-9205, extension 2385

DOLPHIN CONNECTION
OCEAN SEMINAR PROGRAMS

1.   Advanced Ocean Seminars

Recommended prerequisites for your participation:
   a. prior experiences with dolphins in oceans or rivers
   b. able to swim easily in the ocean
   c. previous meditation experience

These Seminars are for people who are already in contact with cetaceans. This is a six day workshop which includes swimming from boats to allow the Spinner Dolphins and Bottlenose Dolphins who live in Hawaii to join us. We spend the largest part of each day on 60 foot sailing vessels. Snorkeling skills are essential. The most advanced cosmological teachings of the dolphins and whales are shared. Co-facilitated by Joan Ocean and John Float.

2.   Joan and the Whales

Join Joan Ocean, the dolphins and the whales for a six day adventure which includes sailing, swimming, toning and meditating among the whales, receiving their frequency-shifting sounds and loving bioluminescence in the warm Hawaiian waters. Accommodations are at luxury oceanfront resorts on the Kona Coast.

3.   Week With Joan Ocean

Live in the fourth and fifth Dimension for a week while swimming among dolphins and experiencing Joan's new work of progressing into the Future. View the world of 2011 and see clearly your spiritual purposes for being here during this time of Great Transition. Daily meditations and the use of dolphin whole-brain, neuro-sonic harmonies to journey into higher aspects of ourselves and our expanded world. Accommodations are in oceanfront homes. Swim skills are required.

4.   Ocean Seminar One Programs

The original life-changing Seminar created by Joan Ocean and now facilitated by Trish Regan and Doug Hackett. For beginner dolphin swimmers and meditators.

5.   Cetacean Celebration

An annual gathering of human and dolphin pods for swimming, dancing, singing and sharing. Everyone is invited to Hawaii for this joyful celebration.

**For information about dolphin and whale Seminars
in Hawaii and other locations:
Phone and Fax in Hawaii, USA: 808-323-9605**

A Dolphin Connection Book